The History of the United States

A Captivating Guide to American History, Including Events Such as the American Revolution, French and Indian War, Boston Tea Party, Pearl Harbor, and the Gulf War

Free Bonus from Captivating History
(Available for a Limited time)

Hi History Lovers!

Now you have a chance to join our exclusive history list so you can get your first history ebook for free as well as discounts and a potential to get more history books for free! Simply visit the link below to join.

Captivatinghistory.com/ebook

Also, make sure to follow us on Facebook, Twitter and Youtube by searching for Captivating History.

We here highly resolve that these dead shall not have died in vain—that this nation, under God, shall have a new birth of freedom—and that government of the people, by the people, for the people, shall not perish from the earth.

- Abraham Lincoln, Gettysburg Address, 1863

Contents

Introduction

When the first settlers reached the United States of America and started to chip out a living in the wilderness that seemed so fierce and unfamiliar to their European eyes, they could never have dreamed that someday the land upon which they stood would become one of the most powerful countries in the entire world. When Native Americans first witnessed those white sails bringing ships with white sailors into their world for the first time, they could never have dreamed that within a few centuries their population would be all but destroyed, that they would have to endure massacre after massacre, be stripped of their freedom and confined to comparatively tiny reservations, and walk the Trail of Tears within the next few hundred years.

When colonial America clashed with France in the French and Indian War, and Great Britain jumped in to rescue its colonies from the struggle, it could never have dreamed that within a few decades, Americans would revolt against Great Britain itself, throw off its shackles, and declare itself an independent country with its own ideas. When George Washington first carried the message that would precipitate the French and Indian War to its French recipient, a twenty-one-year-old riding through wild territory in falling snow, he could never have dreamed that one day he would become the first president of the United States.

When the preachers of the Great Awakening stood on the backs of wagons or bits of old tree stumps and told the American people a new story of individual freedom and the power of ordinary people, they could never have dreamed that their preaching would trigger a landslide of abolitionism that would end in a civil war that almost tore the entire country apart. When the Civil War was finally won by the Union, and all African Americans' chains were broken at last, the military leaders could never have dreamed that within the next half century, the United States would emerge as one of the world's greatest military powers during the Spanish-American War. And when those soldiers won the struggle against Spain in Cuba, they could never have dreamed that later in the century, Cuba itself would turn against them and become the single greatest threat of nuclear annihilation during the Cold War.

When the Wright Brothers first took to the air and Thomas Edison made the lightbulb, they could never have dreamed that American innovation would produce not only the Ford car, basketball, the telephone, and Facebook, but it would also be instrumental in creating the atomic bombs that killed hundreds of thousands of people and finally brought an end to the Second World War. As for Martin Luther King, Jr., he did dream. He had a dream of equality and brotherhood, and his dream at least partially came true in 2008 when America saw the inauguration of its first black president. Never could the slaves of the great plantations of the South have dreamed that that day would ever come, but it did.

Nobody could have dreamed it, but it all came to pass, and it became the history of the United States of America. And this is how it all happened.

Chapter 1 – The People Who Were There First

Talapas made the world. He created the surface of the earth, building rivers and mountains, trees and hills, rocks and streams. Then he populated the earth with the Totem Spirits—creatures that were partly living and partly spirit.

One of these creatures was the T'soona, or the Thunderbird. It sprang from the back of a fish when the South Wind used his knife to cut the fish the wrong way. Thunderbird leapt forth from the cut and flew up into the air, and the span of its wings was enough to blot out the sun. The sound of its wings was a terrible roar, the flash of its eyes deadly and frightening.

Talapas ordered the Thunderbird to fly to Saddleback Mountain— Kaheese, in the mother tongue. Obediently, the great bird did so. When it reached the mountain, it squatted down and laid five giant, magical eggs before flying away.

It was at this point that a vengeful Giantess arrived. The Giantess had warned the South Wind not to cut the fish sideways instead of down the length of its spine, and she had seen the result of his refusal to heed her warning. Now, she was determined to take and eat the eggs of the Thunderbird. Seizing one, she threw it angrily down the mountain—but she didn't get much further with her quest. With a terrible cry, a great, burning creature swept down out of the sky, its feathers ablaze. It was the Spirit Bird, and it was determined to protect the eggs of the Thunderbird. Swooping down, it set the Giantess alight with its burning wings. Ignited, burning, and screaming, she fell down the side of the mountain, and that was the end of her.

As for the eggs of the Thunderbird, they were safely left on Saddleback Mountain. And when they hatched, the people—the T'sinuk—emerged onto the earth that Talapas made.

- Chinook creation myth

Like the rest of the New World, North America was not unpopulated when the Europeans first arrived. In fact, there were several diverse and complicated cultures residing on the continent by Columbus' arrival in the 15th century, each with their own way of life.

The Origins of the Native Americans

People likely first arrived in North America during the Ice Age. Crossing the Bering Strait, which would have been frozen over at this point, they probably originated in Asia and first set foot in Alaska. Several waves of migrations brought groups of people into North America, taking them through Canada and down into the area that is now the United States. Over time, they expanded into hundreds of different tribes. By 1000 BCE, they had covered the entire continent. The Americas may have been labeled "the New World" by its European discoverers, but in reality, they had been well explored for thousands of years by the time of their arrival.

In fact, by the end of the 15th century, there were millions of native people living all over North America. Some estimates put their population as high as eighteen million—six times the population of England and Wales at that time. By sharp contrast, less than five and a half million Native Americans populate the United States today.

The Earliest Native Americans

Some of the earliest evidence of human activity in North America is actually located on its southern end: New Mexico. Here, the Clovis tribe was one of the first cultures to make their marks on history. During a time when the Columbian mammoth still roamed the earth, this tribe learned how to hunt these behemoths for their hides and meat. A single mammoth could feed an entire village for some time, but bringing it down was not a task for the faint of heart—or for the ill-equipped. In order to be able to hunt these creatures, the Clovis tribe crafted what was probably the first American invention: the Clovis point.

These stone knives were usually carved from jasper, flint, or obsidian, and the workmanship of these points is exquisite. They were designed to be mounted on a shaft to form a deadly and razor-sharp spear that could cut through the mammoth's tough hide. In fact, the Clovis points were so good at what they did that they contributed to the mammoth's untimely demise: these majestic creatures slowly became extinct after the arrival of humans in North America, partially because of habitat loss, but also due to hunting.

Another culture, about three hundred years after the Clovis tribe, emerged in a similar area and with a similar goal. While the mammoth was probably mostly extinct by the time of the Folsom people, they had another large animal to hunt—a species of giant bison. These were faster and more agile than the mammoths, and the spears that the Clovis people had invented were too cumbersome for hunting them. Instead, improving on the Clovis design, the Folsom people developed a device known as an *atlatl*. It could launch a spear much farther and faster than a human arm, allowing its user to bring down the mighty bison.

Migrating into the Great Plains, the native peoples continued to hunt bison, structuring much of their culture around their huge prey; they became nomads who followed the bison herds wherever they went, abandoning their farms and relying on the herds for their prey. This culture would endure for centuries, continuing even after the arrival of the Europeans drove the Native Americans onto small reservations. Millennia before the Europeans arrived, though, the Plano culture was already refining its hunting techniques specifically for the bison. It was this tribe that developed the technique of driving a herd of bison off a cliff in order to kill large amounts of them with less effort.

The Plano culture would also develop new ways of preserving and cooking food. They used stones to grind up grains into a kind of coarse flour, also producing the first "ground beef"—mashed-up bison meat—in this way. The first preserved "beef" was also made by the Plano; while a far cry from modern beef jerky, their dried balls of fat and protein were a nutritious source of long-lasting food in times when hunting was poor.

Along the coast of the Northwest, however, multiple tribes were exploring another way of life: fishing and boating. The ancestors of tribes such as the Haida, Nootka, and Tlingit, these peoples embraced a far more complicated culture. Not only did they build beautiful canoes and hunt sea creatures as big as whales, but they also worked in something that resembled the European feudal system, with chiefs functioning as nobility, presiding over commoners and even slaves. Pride was an integral part of their culture; wealth was seen as a defining symbol of status, and they went to extensive lengths to show off their material gains by throwing elaborate parties for their friends and neighbors. They also built wooden houses and were excellent woodworkers, yet these tribes did not farm or have any concept of agriculture.

Some of the first farmers were the Adena culture, who lived around 1000 BCE. As well as growing many of the crops that American farmers still produce today—such as corn and sunflowers—they also had elaborate burial rituals that involved building huge mounds, possibly including the Great Serpent Mound, in which to bury their dead. The Great Serpent Mound is a mysterious archaeological wonder that has been puzzling historians for centuries. Certainly built by some Native American tribe, this is an effigy mound, built to resemble an animal that possibly had some spiritual significance. Despite being only three feet high, it's almost 1,350 feet long, and its sinuous curves are surprisingly symmetrical. It may have been built either by the Adena or by the Fort Ancients, who lived in the same area over a millennium later.

Native Americans at the Arrival of Columbus

By the late 1400s, when Spanish ships first set sail in the hopes of finding a new route to India, the Native American population was as complicated as it was proliferating. Each tribe had a complete and independent culture whose lives were not that different from those of the Europeans who were about to invade them. Like the Europeans, the Native Americans had cities, trade routes, villages, complicated social structures, rulers, wars among themselves, and hundreds of different languages. They had domesticated several different types of animals, including dogs, turkeys, guinea pigs, and llamas, although the horse was a creature utterly unknown to them—modern horses would only arrive in North America during the sixteenth century.

They also had various belief systems and creation stories which differed from tribe to tribe. Most of these were rooted and aligned in nature. The tribes had been existing closely with plants, animals, and the environment for centuries; they worshiped some creatures as spirits, while others were revered and respected as food sources. Gods were still a part of their religions, usually with multiple gods governed over by a leading creator spirit. Some Native Americans today still practice their ancient cultural beliefs, and the imprint of these beliefs remains in the country in the form of mounds and totem poles.

While there were squabbles among the tribes, and war undoubtedly being a part of their lives, the Native Americans had been existing in relative peace and isolation for thousands of years. All that was about to change. The Europeans were coming, and they would bring with them a level of death, war, and disease that the natives had never had to contend with before.

Chapter 2 – A Time of Exploration

Illustration I: A copy of a John White watercolor, painted in 1590, showing Native Americans building a dugout canoe

Christopher Columbus did not discover North America.

In fact, the first Europeans to reach North America were probably the Vikings. Leif Erikson, the son of Erik the Red, likely reached

Canada in the late 10th century; he spent several months there and may have explored the coast all the way down to the modern-day Bahamas, although there is little evidence to support this claim.

The European Discovery of North America

By the time Christopher Columbus reached Hispaniola in 1492, the Vikings were long gone. Columbus was the first European to actually colonize the Americas; when Columbus returned to Europe, he left a small garrison of men behind on an island known, at the time, as San Salvador. This was the beginnings of the colonization of the New World.

Columbus himself never actually reached what is now the United States. In fact, for the rest of his life, he would remain in denial that he had discovered a new continent at all; he firmly believed that he had succeeded in his goal of finding a new route to Asia, and thus named the natives of the area "Indians," a label that has stuck to this day. While Columbus explored the islands and the mainland of South America, it was a relatively unknown Italian explorer, working for the English, who would land on North America: John Cabot.

We might not celebrate Cabot Day the way we celebrate Columbus Day, but Cabot, in 1497, was the first European since Leif Erikson to reach mainland North America. Commissioned by King Henry VII of England, Cabot's life and voyages are wreathed in mystery. His goal was the same as that of Columbus—to establish a trade route to India—but he believed that sailing farther north would achieve the goal of reaching Asia without having to circumnavigate Africa. When he landed on Newfoundland in June 1497, he, too, believed that he had found a route to India. He named several of the surrounding islands with a distinctly patriotic British flavor, such as the Island of St. John and England's Cape. Returning to the English king to report the happy news, he attempted a second voyage in 1498, and it is thought that he died in a shipwreck.

Spaniards in America

In 1513, the Spanish—who were in the process of subduing Hispaniola, Puerto Rico, Cuba, and other islands of the Caribbean—made their first foray into mainland North America. Led by Juan Ponce de León, who had previously been the governor of Puerto Rico, they landed in modern-day Florida. The swampy, wild marshlands could not have looked that much different from the jungles of South America; in fact, at the time, the explorers likely did not make any distinction between the place they'd just landed in and those they'd already seen. There was no way that they could have known that they were standing on ground that would someday belong to one of the greatest powers in the modern world.

Ponce de León, unlike Cabot and Columbus, was not searching for a way to get to Asia. Material wealth had little appeal to him; instead, according to legend, he himself was searching for something legendary and far more mystical, a concept that had been luring men from all walks of life for centuries: The Fountain of Youth. This fountain was supposed to produce magical water that could reverse the aging process and allow people to live forever.

Searching diligently for the fountain, Ponce de León explored most of Florida's coastline, even naming the peninsula (which he took to be an island) after a Spanish feast known as *Pascua Florida*. The name stuck, and in 1521, Ponce de León returned with a group of men who wanted to colonize the "island." Their efforts were met with strenuous resistance. News of the horrible fates that had been suffered by other natives had reached the Native Americans residing in Florida, and they put up an unexpected fight, wounding Ponce de León so severely that his men had to retreat. He died in Cuba, unable to recover from the injuries he had received in the battle. There would be no Fountain of Youth for this intrepid explorer; instead, he succumbed at the age of 61 to an arrow in the thigh.

French Expeditions

Starting with a voyage in 1524 by Giovanni da Verrazano, the French started to stake their claim in the northern parts of what is now the United States. While the Spanish were controlling Florida and moving ever northward, it was Verrazano—Italian-born, but employed by France—who became one of the first Europeans to lay eyes on the bay that would eventually become New York Harbor.

Jacques Cartier, who is thought to have been with Verrazano on his expedition sailing around modern-day North Carolina and New York, made a second French-funded voyage to North America in 1534. He, too, was seeking passage to Asia; instead, he stumbled upon what has now become Canada, staking the first real French claim in North America, one that would last for centuries.

Verrazano was not the only Italian-born sailor who would leave his mark on the New World and its history. Amerigo Vespucci, a Florentine in the service of Spain, would later claim to have discovered the South American mainland long before Columbus did. History has since proven that Vespucci certainly did not see the mainland before at least 1499, and even this is dubious. Nevertheless, he was believed for long enough that the New World took its name from his own first name: America, after Amerigo.

The Lost Colony

Ultimately, although Spain was actively exploring in the south and France in the north, it would be the English whose grip on the modern-day United States would last the longest of all—and it all started with the Lost Colony.

John White, an English explorer funded by Sir Walter Raleigh (Queen Elizabeth I's favorite adventurer and scoundrel), is thought to have made his first voyage, led by Philip Amadas and Arthur Barlowe, to the New World in 1584, landing near what is now North Carolina. He would return again a year later in a mission that almost killed both him and his men when they made enemies of the natives by murdering one of their leaders. Miraculously, the raiding and marauding Sir Francis Drake—a buccaneer in the service of the queen—stumbled upon the survivors on the shore of Roanoke Island.

Undeterred, White was determined to give his queen a claim to the endless resources of the New World. Legends and stories of mystical treasures and abundant riches filled this era: The Fountain of Youth, a city made entirely of gold, a passage to Asia—the attractions of the New World were both real and legendary. And the British wanted a piece of it. In 1587, White was back, this time to establish a more secure and permanent colony. He brought more than one hundred people to Roanoke Island, including women and children, and they started to build a village. It was here that the first English child was born in North America: Virginia Dare, a little girl named after the surrounding land which Walter Raleigh had named Virginia for England's virgin queen.

This time, White was wise enough not to treat the natives violently. Instead, the Europeans became firm friends with the nearby Croatan tribe; so much so that White himself would paint a series of famous watercolors of these natives. His paintings became the first portrayals of Native Americans that the English back home would ever see.

However, all was still not well with the colony. Supplies started to run low; the English had not yet learned how to survive in America the way the natives did, and before the year was over, White was sailing back to England to gather what was needed to keep the colony healthy. The plan was simply to gather the necessities and sail back as quickly as possible. It was not to be. The Anglo-Spanish War broke out as White arrived back home, turning the waters surrounding the two countries into an open war zone. To sail through it was to invite disaster. Agonizingly, White was stuck in England, utterly unable to contact the settlers he had left behind on Roanoke. And his daughter, Eleanor Dare, and her newborn daughter, little Virginia, were among them.

Three long years dragged past. Three years during which Eleanor could have had no way of knowing what had happened to her father. Did she presume him lost at sea? Killed by pirates? Did she wonder, in the dark moments, if he had simply left her behind to die? It was none of the above, and in 1590, White was finally able to set sail for Roanoke once more. He couldn't wait to see his daughter and to hold his little grandchild in his arms again.

He never would. All that was left of the colony was the word "Croatoan" carved into a wooden post. Whether the word referred to the native tribe living nearby or to a neighboring island, White would never know. Funding for the expedition had run out. He had to return to England, his ships full of supplies and his heart stripped bare, and to this day, no one really knows what happened to the Lost Colony.

Chapter 3 – Colonizing America

Despite the failure that was the Lost Colony, England would still be one of the first countries to establish a permanent colony in North America—and it wasn't far from Roanoke Island itself.

The fervor to colonize the New World sprang not only from a spirit of adventure but also from desperation and necessity. England itself was changing, enduring a time of religious and economic turmoil. To put it simply, England just wasn't big enough for all of its people. The fact that firstborn sons generally inherited the entire estate left many younger sons seeking their fortune; worse, an economic recession had plunged the lower classes into poverty, and the island was struggling to support its ever-growing population. With home no longer welcoming to them, the English started to set their sights further afield. And surrounded by its legends of gold and freedom, the New World seemed like the ideal solution for the adventurers among England's desperate.

It was not only the poverty-stricken, however, that sought wonders and riches in America. King James I himself was watching with trepidation as the Spanish continued to expand their claims in North America. He knew that the entire New World might slip out of his grip if he didn't do something, and so, he granted a charter for Virginia—the area that Walter Raleigh's mission had claimed for England several decades ago—to be thoroughly explored and colonized in 1606.

Jamestown

The Virginia Company of London was a joint-stock company that received the charter to explore Virginia, and it wasted no time in putting together an expedition. Like the fateful journey that Columbus took more than a hundred years earlier when he first stumbled upon the Americas, this voyage would be undertaken in three ships. *Susan Constant*, *Discovery*, and *Godspeed* arrived in Virginia in 1607. They brought with them 104 English men and boys, led by a council that the Virginia Company had elected. Edward Maria Wingfield was the first president of the colony, but it quickly became apparent that another council member—ex-soldier John Smith—was the real leader of the group. His stern leadership and willingness to bargain and cooperate with the natives went a long way toward keeping the colony alive as they began to build their first settlement. This was named Jamestown, after the king that had sent them there.

The settlers would soon discover why it had taken so long for any colony to be established on the North American mainland. For a start, the continent's human population had been sealed off from the rest of the world for thousands of years, resulting in diseases that were utterly alien to the European immune system. There was no real way of treating these illnesses, and so, they spread like wildfire among the colonists, causing many deaths.

It would also soon become evident that the land the Native Americans found so abundant would prove to be a barren and fruitless wasteland to the English. It had been centuries, and many generations, since the English had had to live off the land; their book knowledge was no good to them now, as they were faced with the reality of needing to hunt and gather in order to survive. Despite assistance from the local Powhatan tribe—who sent food parcels as gifts despite generally keeping their distance from the settlers—the colonists gradually began to starve.

The Starving Time

The situation grew dire in the winter of 1609. For three long years, the colonists had been scraping by, barely able to maintain their settlement, struggling to even stay alive. By the end of the year, about 90% of the original colonists were dead. Only a tiny handful remained, clinging to life and disillusioned as their dreams of gold had been frosted away by the reality of the winter. Worse, they were no longer friendly with the Powhatan. Their only real source of reliable food had dried up; they feared for their lives to go outside, leaving them in a kind of passive, desperate siege inside their settlement. Boot leather and dead bodies had to do for food. The period was known, with simple despair, as the Starving Time.

A new fleet of settlers had been sent to join those already in Jamestown, but a shipwreck had landed them on Bermuda, trapped and unable to reach their fellow colonists. It was only in the spring that they would finally be able to finish building some new boats and sail over to the mainland, where they found the wild-eyed survivors starving and desperate. The decision was made to abandon Jamestown and flee back home—even the turbulent English economy was better than being shot by Indian arrows out in the unknown wilderness. Jamestown was abandoned, but when word arrived of another relief fleet making its way to the shore, the settlers returned.

The Peace-Seeking Powhatan

Once the new governor of Jamestown, Thomas West, Lord De La Warr, had arrived, things began to look up a little for the settlers. John Rolfe—a businessman who had been one of those who survived the shipwreck and made it from Bermuda to Jamestown—came up with the first cash crop that the Virginia Company had been desperately looking for: tobacco. The first crop was planted in 1611, and resources slowly began trickling back into the settlement.

Relations with the Powhatan tribe, however, began to worsen. Raids were launched on the villages, stealing food and supplies. As superior as the Powhatan were in their knowledge of survival in the woods, they could not match the English in terms of warfare. Wielding bows and arrows, they struggled to fight the English and their guns.

Prior to leaving Virginia in 1609, John Smith occasionally led these raids, yet he seemed to be seeking a different solution at one point. Eventually, Powhatan Chief Wahunsenacawh befriended Smith and bestowed upon him the title of werowance, the leader of the colonists as recognized by the Powhatan. He became a liaison between the Powhatan and the English, if an imperfect one, often reverting to raids if the Powhatan did not provide as much food as was demanded.

The situation remained tenuous until 1614 when a strange new union would bring about a kind of peace. Pocahontas, the teenage daughter of Wahunsenacawh, had been kidnapped by English soldiers. Her husband, Kocoum, had been killed during the kidnapping, and her baby stripped out of her arms. However, she would soon meet John Rolfe, the man who had started the tobacco crops. Whether they fell in love or whether Rolfe recognized the importance of an alliance with the Powhatan at this stage is uncertain; either way, he took her out of captivity and married her in 1614. Pocahontas became Rebecca Rolfe, and peace was established between the two nations until her death in 1617.

By that time, Jamestown had been firmly established as an English colony. Women had crossed the Atlantic and either brought their families with them or started new ones when they arrived; Africans were shipped over to work on the tobacco plantations, and the English grip on North America was starting to look permanent.

Other Colonies

With Jamestown starting to flourish, other nations were hot on the British heels to establish permanent colonies on the North American continent. The Dutch, Spanish, and French had already been fishing and exploring the lands and waters of the New World for decades; now, they started to build permanent settlements of their own.

As early as 1608, the French had built their first settlement: Quebec in modern-day Canada. The Spanish, who had started to work in California and Texas as well as New Mexico, were more focused on sending Catholic missionaries to work with the natives, although their settlement of St. Augustine, built in 1565, would grow into the oldest continuously inhabited city in North America.

The Dutch West India Company was also interested in lands and resources in North America. Dutch colonists lived mainly in what was then known as New Netherland, now New York, with their first settlement being founded in 1614.

Many of the first colonists came to the New World fleeing religious persecution. Puritans and French Huguenots arrived in droves. A group of Huguenots who attempted to settle in Florida in 1564 were one of the first European groups to establish a colony; their attempt was ill-fated, however, as the Spaniards who controlled the area quickly discovered and killed them all. The Pilgrims, English Puritans who arrived in 1620 aboard the famous *Mayflower*, were more fortunate. They established Plymouth in modern-day New England.

By 1700, thousands of colonists from all over Europe had arrived in North America and established roots there despite the odds, and the English population of North America numbered a quarter of a million. Some attempted to coexist with the natives, others fought them, and most of them accidentally killed hundreds of them with European diseases for which the natives had no immunity. The colonists battled with disease and a climate that was utterly alien to them, but gradually more and more of them arrived and hung on. The colonists came from all walks of life, all sorts of religious convictions, and many different countries, but they had one thing in common: they were determined to build a life for themselves in the New World, no matter the cost to them.

And no matter the cost to others.

Chapter 4 – The French and Indian War

Wherever people went, war came with them.

The Native American tribes had been skirmishing among one another for generations. When the Europeans arrived, raids and small struggles began almost immediately, and it's not hard to see why. What has now been called "colonization" must have looked, to the Native American eye, like nothing short of an invasion. While some Native American tribes were welcoming, and some Europeans were interested in learning and cooperating with their strange new neighbors, tension was widespread, and fighting became the general rule.

It was the Pilgrims that established Plymouth that signed the first peace treaty between Europeans and Native Americans. These 101 Puritans who arrived from England in 1620 found themselves in what appeared to be a paradise of green fields and clear streams— and introduced to a strange new people whose culture, language, and beliefs were completely different to those of the Pilgrims. The Wampanoags were just as suspicious of the Pilgrims as the Pilgrims were of them, but by March 1621, they were able to put aside their differences long enough to sign a peace treaty whose terms were as simple as they were fair. The treaty vowed that the two nations would do one another no harm, and any who violated the terms of the treaty would be turned over to the opposite nation in order to be punished according to their customs. The terms were strict enough that the treaty held for almost a century.

European War Spills into North America

The first war involving Europeans that took place in North America was not between Europeans and natives but rather a continuation of a great conflict that was consuming the entirety of Europe.

In 1739, near the shores of Cuba, a Spanish soldier boarded the ship of English merchant Robert Jenkins. Simmering tensions between Spain and England led the Spaniard to use his cutlass to cut off the merchant's ear, returning the severed organ to its owner and telling him to take it back to the English king. Jenkins did so, leading to the uniquely-named War of Jenkins' Ear. When the War of the Austrian Succession flared in 1740, it had already assimilated the War of Jenkins' Ear and dragged most of the powers of Europe into a messy fight that eventually spilled over in all directions.

For North Americans, this distant war would come to the colonies with a sharp reality. The French, English, Spanish, and Dutch had been coexisting more or less peacefully for more than a century, being more preoccupied with other problems—such as skirmishing with the natives, surviving alien American diseases, and eking out an existence on the face of a sometimes hostile new continent—but things changed suddenly as King George's War began in 1744. Not as much a separate war as simply the American theater of the War of the Austrian Succession, it pitted the French and English against one another. Its most major action was the capture of Louisbourg, a French fortress located on the Cape Breton Island in Nova Scotia, Canada. The French put great trust in Louisbourg as being their strongest fortress, and when the British captured it in 1745 after a six-week siege in which both sides suffered heavy losses, they were infuriated.

The war ended in 1748 with a treaty that effectively tried to reverse the war—most possessions were returned to their countries according to the way it had been before the war broke out. To the American colonists fighting on the British side, it seemed a cruel and unnecessary thing to strip their hard-won Louisbourg from them and hand it back to the French. They had lost hundreds of good men in the fight to get their hands on the fortress; now, a bunch of men who had likely never even seen battle, sitting in some cozy parlor thousands of miles away, had taken it away from them for no reason that they could understand. It was one of the first blows that would eventually sever Britain and America from one another.

First, though, the animosity between British and French colonies in North America would have to be dealt with – and struggles with the natives were becoming more frequent and violent. The French and Indian War was imminent.

A Warning to the French

The young major had to pull his hat down low over his eyes against the driving snow that howled over the landscape with a vengeful fury, throwing fistfuls of ice against his neck and pushing its cold fingers down the collar of his red coat as he steered his horse down into the Ohio River Valley. He knew that this was some of the most fertile land in North America, greatly valued by British Americans for its good soil and easy access to the Ohio River, which allowed them to transport goods by boat down to the Mississippi for trading. But now, it looked like a barren wasteland of ice and rock. His horse had to tread carefully as it made its way out of British territory and up toward the French-controlled Fort LeBoeuf.

The major was only twenty-one years old, and he was gripped by both fear and excitement as he looked up at the French fortress. It was December 1753, and he had been sixteen years old when King George's War—the latest conflict between the French and English forces—had ended. He remembered it all too well, and despite the signed treaty forming a tenuous barrier between the opposing nations, he still saw the French as the enemy. Especially now that he had been sent here by his commanding officer to deliver a warning. He touched his chest pocket as his horse made its way to the fortress gates, feeling the letter nestled there. Virginia Lt. Governor Robert Dinwiddie had composed the message to warn the French to stay out of British-controlled areas in the valley, and the young major knew that if the French resisted, Dinwiddie would be ready for battle. After all, the British Americans numbered about two million at the time; the French, less than one hundred thousand.

To his surprise, he was warmly received into the fortress. Grooms rushed out to take his horse, and after he had declared his business, he was ushered into a warm room where a blazing fire crackled in the hearth. Warming his blue hands by the flames, the major tried to control his nerves. This would be the first real military mission he had ever been sent on, and he was determined not to let Dinwiddie down.

A Frenchman walked into the room and came over to the major, smiling peacefully and extending a friendly hand. "Captain Jacques Legardeur de Saint-Pierre," he introduced himself.

Fearlessly returning the captain's smile, the major gripped his hand. "Major George Washington."

The War Begins

The delivery of the message from Dinwiddie was one of George Washington's very first missions, and while he succeeded in the delivery, the message did not have its intended effect. Saint-Pierre's response to Dinwiddie was dismissive, claiming that the French king had every right to British lands in the Ohio River Valley. In 1754, Dinwiddie declared war on the French, and a long struggle began.

Despite the fact that the French were hugely outnumbered by the English, they enjoyed early military successes due to their alliances with the natives of the area. This is why the war is known as the French and Indian War, particularly in America. In Britain, the war

dressed differently, and most of them had never even seen Great Britain itself. Yet there were no British Americans in Parliament, and Parliament made all their choices for them.

Since the French and Indian War, these choices largely consisted of increasing taxes. First, a heavy tax was imposed on all printed paper, from books to newspapers to postage stamps. Then, worse, essentials were being taxed—glass, lead, and even tea. The taxes led to unrest throughout Boston, and this unrest led to thousands of British soldiers pouring into the city to quell the voices of the citizens. Even merchants and shop owners selling British wares came under fire from unhappy citizens and retaliated with violence.

The Boston Massacre

March 5th, 1770, was an icy day. The streets of Boston were coated in snow and ice; where Private Hugh White stood on guard in front of the Custom House, he could see his breath steaming in the air in front of him. The cold was not the only thing that made the atmosphere seem tense. He knew that there had been chaos throughout the city for months. What he didn't know was that he was about to become the unwitting trigger for the worst violence yet.

As Private White stood outside the Custom House, he knew he was guarding money that was almost all destined for Great Britain. With Boston being a port town, its economy depended heavily on trade, and much of the profits from that trade went straight to the coffers of the British king. The colonists saw the Custom House as a blight on their city, a place where stolen money was hoarded before being shipped back to their oppressor. And on this evening, a handful of men decided that they could no longer take it lying down. Appearing in the streets and from the surrounding buildings, the group of colonists started to mock and insult Private White. Shaking their fists at him, they threatened to beat him up and to storm the Custom House and take back what was rightfully theirs.

Private White tried to stand his ground, but eventually, he was overwhelmed. The crowd was pressing thick upon White and his compatriots, and colonists had even begun poking the soldiers to get a rise out of them. And a rise they got when one of the soldiers struck back, hitting one of the colonists in the head with his musket. Blood spilled onto the snow, and as the red droplets splattered on the white ground, something snapped in the atmosphere. The colonists started to throw rocks, sticks, and snowballs at the British soldier; he shouted and gestured wildly with his bayonet, and soon the air was thick with shouting and swearing, cursing and panicking. All over the city, warning bells began to ring, calling more and more colonists out onto the street. Soon, they gathered enough courage to storm White, threatening further violence. He had had enough. He called for reinforcements.

They arrived in the form of Captain Thomas Preston and a group of British soldiers who surged to the defense of their comrade. Usually, the arrival of a mass of angry soldiers was enough to quell a riot, but not today. Incensed, the colonists fell upon the British, knocking one down along with his weapon. It is believed that the fallen soldier fired into the crowd, and after a moment of silence, more soldiers fired as well, despite no order being given to do so. Bullets burst through the air, punching through flesh, splattering blood, as screams of pain and anger filled the crowd. Chaos erupted. The colonists fell upon the soldiers with clubs and sticks; the soldiers fired back, and for a few mad seconds, the streets became a bloodbath.

When it was all over, five colonists were dead. The soldiers escaped with only minor injuries, a fact that was seized upon by propaganda fueled by an angered colony that felt it had been unjustly dealt with. Anti-British sentiment spread like wildfire throughout the city. The Bostonians had had enough.

The Tea Act

One of the heaviest taxes Great Britain had imposed on America involved the Tea Act of 1773. The Boston Massacre, among other things, had eventually persuaded Britain to withdraw some of its heavier taxes, but a heavy tax on tea remained, and in 1773, this was made worse when the British East India Company was effectively given a monopoly on the tea trade since the Tea Act allowed it to sell Chinese tea duty-free. This proved lucrative for the company and for Great Britain but disastrous for independent American merchants hoping to sell their own tea. Since they were subjected to the taxes, their tea was vastly more expensive than the British East India Company's tea, and so, most Americans had no choice but to purchase the British tea even though it was crippling the local economy.

This act was protested by a group of revolutionaries known as the Sons of Liberty. Founded to protest the Stamp Act originally, they continued to push back against British oppression. Led by a man named Samuel Adams, the revolutionaries held rallies and protests throughout the city. And their biggest protest would occur on December 16th, 1773. Three ships—the *Dartmouth*, the *Eleanor*, and the *Beaver*—had arrived in Griffin's Wharf laden with British East India Company tea.

The Boston Tea Party

The vast cargoes of tea provided a tipping point for the enraged citizens of Boston. Gathering in the thousands at the wharf, their protest was vehement enough that a meeting was called at the Old South Meeting House to hear the colonists' opinion on the newly arrived tea. Their vote was almost unanimous: the tea should not be sold or even unloaded in Boston; it should be thrown away or sent back to Great Britain, just as long as it ceased to undermine their local economy.

Their vote was met with almost instant dismissal. Governor Thomas Hutchison brushed them off and ordered the tea to be unloaded. Colonial workers refused to touch it, and soon a plan was made to ensure that none of that tea would ever be drunk in Boston.

As darkness fell over the wharf, a group of men began to gather on a nearby hilltop. Despite the eagle feathers that bristled across the group and the flash of moonlight off tomahawks clutched in desperate hands, none of them were Native Americans. They were colonists from Boston, disguised as Mohawk warriors, and they were determined to wreak havoc on that tea.

The group numbered somewhere between 30 and 130 men; the harbor was surrounded by British warships. The odds were insurmountable, but the colonists' anger was undeterred by danger. When night had enveloped the harbor completely, they stormed the ships. Rushing aboard, spurred on by shouts from their commander, the colonists smashed the padlocks and yanked open the hatches of the ships, plunging into their cargo holds. 342 chests of tea—a cargo that would have been worth more than a million dollars today—lay waiting for them. One by one, the chests were heaved onto the deck, split open with the tomahawks, and then tossed overboard. In the lantern light, tea leaves floated all over the harbor in the millions, each representing lost money for the British East India Company and the British Crown. Each was a triumph for the rebels, who whooped war cries as they flung the chests overboard. Splashes and shouts filled the night, and yet no attempt was made to stop them.

By the end of the night, every last one of the tea chests had been thrown into the harbor. No one was harmed, but the colonists' statement was made perfectly clear: they were done with British taxes.

The Intolerable Acts

Despite the lack of violence, the British would be equally clear in their response to the protest that has gone down in history as the Boston Tea Party. In 1774, only months after the protest, a series of new acts were passed that the British called the Coercive Acts and the Americans called the Intolerable Acts. Either way, they were designed to crush the Americans' spirit, and they blatantly sought to strip power from the colonists. The Quebec Act guaranteed that the colonists of the province of Quebec, just north of Ohio, could freely practice the Catholic faith—something that was deeply offensive to the mainly Puritan colonists. The Boston Port Act closed Boston's harbor to trade, stripping the city of much of its income; the Massachusetts Government Act granted greater power to its British governor; the Quartering Act demanded that colonists freely provide barracks to British troops; and the Administration of Justice Act ordered that trials against government officials would all be held in Great Britain, making it practically impossible for colonists to testify against any officials.

The acts were unfair. But like so many attempts made by tyrants to redouble their grip upon the rising spirit of a revolution, they were also utterly unsuccessful. A new era was coming.

Chapter 6 – The American Revolution

And yet, through the gloom and the light,

The fate of a nation was riding that night;

And the spark struck out by that steed, in his flight,

Kindled the land into flame with its heat.

- Henry Wadsworth Longfellow, "Paul Revere's Ride"

In the dark night of April 18th, 1775, a brown horse flew through the darkness, urged on by a desperate rider who clutched the reins in trembling hands as he mustered the surrounding countryside to battle. The rider was Paul Revere; the horse, a mare named Brown Beauty, a mare whose legs would bear her and her rider an epic distance that night as Revere sought to warn the patriots of Middlesex that a mass of British soldiers had arrived and was marching across the countryside to attack Concord. The British came in determined ranks, their red coats ablaze in the light of every lantern they passed. And ahead of them rode a series of courageous men on horseback, riding like the wind in order to bring the news of the invasion to their fellow rebels.

The Battles of Lexington and Concord

Revere and the other riders achieved their mission, even though some were thrown from their horses and Revere himself was briefly captured and detained at Lexington. Despite the mishaps that befell some of the riders, others got through and brought word to the Middlesex towns about the British attack.

By the time the advance guard of nearly 240 British soldiers arrived in Lexington, the rebels were ready for them. A militia of 77 men had been gathered on the town green in a peaceful show of force, and when the mighty British army appeared on the hilltop, the British commander cried, "Throw down your arms! Ye villains! Ye rebels!"

The rebellious spirit in these men must have given the British army pause, as they stood on the green gazing up at an enemy over three times their size. But they knew that to attack now would be foolhardy. Their commander gave them the order to disperse, but his shouting was half-drowned out by the yelling British. Confused, only some of the militia broke their ranks while others milled around or prepared for battle.

Then, a shot rang out. A terrible crack, followed by the smell of gun smoke. History has not been able to explain who exactly fired that first shot, but fired it was, and it sowed chaos among the assembled soldiers. Spooked, the British fired a volley into the militiamen, their musket balls crashing and ripping through the ranks of the rebels. The colonists returned fire, and with that, the American Revolution had begun.

From Lexington to Concord, to Boston to Cambridge, and finally all the way back to Charlestown Neck, the militiamen harried the British, the initial 77 being joined by more than 3,000 others. While at first the British seemed to have the upper hand, they were soon overwhelmed and put to flight by the colonists, finally ending up hiding in Charlestown Neck under the safety of their naval support. The British were thoroughly shaken by this turn of events, not having expected the colonists to be able to put up that much resistance.

The American Revolution

The first major battle of the revolution (the Battle of Bunker Hill) took place on June 17th, 1775, at Breed's Hill. This British bid to force the Americans away from Boston was a dismal failure, and it further bolstered American morale as they sought to drive the British out of the continent that they had now claimed as their own. George Washington himself, now a general, soon led his troops into the fray; by March 1776, he had forced thousands of British troops out of Boston, keeping the city firmly in America's grasp. And following the signing of the Declaration of Independence on July 4th, 1776, the war began in earnest.

Continued American success drove the British back into Canada and New York. Things had been looking promising for the Americans during the spring of 1776, but this state of affairs didn't last long. Great Britain was sending over more and more troops, determined not to lose its claim on the New World; the British army was growing by the day, and throughout the last half of 1776 and 1777, they launched offensives that proved almost too much for the Americans. Washington himself was defeated in five out of six battles. Things were not looking good for America by the fall of 1777 until the tide finally turned at the two Battles of Saratoga. An American force commanded by General Horatio Gates finally bested the English by using marksmanship from the cover of thick woods to pick off the British where they sat in an open field; the British were forced to surrender.

After this, the British desperately sought alliances from other countries, gaining some help from the Hessians. In a strange twist of events, the French colonies—against whom the Americans had fought so hard in the French and Indian War, incurring the very debt that had ignited the Revolution in the first place—became America's allies, declaring war on Britain in 1778.

For the next three years, the war split more or less into two: a frustrating stalemate in the North and a series of hard struggles in the South. Loyalists to the British administration were more numerous in the South than in the North, and much of the South remained under British control until 1781, when General Nathanael Greene finally scored a few victories early in the year that eventually led to most of the South ending up under American control by the end of the year.

The Battle of Yorktown

By September 1781, Lieutenant-General Charles Cornwallis—the commander of the British forces—had only 9,000 troops under his command, compared with Washington's 17,000. He had been driven back to the Yorktown Peninsula in Virginia, some of the very first lands that the British had ever set foot upon when they first came to North America. Now, he was holed up in a fortress with his men, watching Washington advance with a strength and sureness that Cornwallis could no longer equal.

Washington laid siege to Yorktown on September 28th, 1781. The fortress held out for three long weeks before finally surrendering on October 19th. The entire army was handed over to Washington, and with that, the fighting on the continent itself was complete. Small naval battles and local skirmishes with loyalists would still occur, but the war was over, and the world knew it. In 1783, Great Britain finally acknowledged the independence of America with the Treaty of Paris. The Declaration of Independence had been recognized by the world at last.

Chapter 7 – The First President

Illustration III: George Washington by John Trumbull

With the Revolution over, America found itself a newly independent state that had to find a way to govern itself in peace as well as it had proven itself in war. This was no simple task. At the time, most of the world was governed by some form of monarchy; the New World itself was little more than a collection of colonies presided over by some European superpower, and democracy was a concept that had barely even been introduced throughout the rest of the world. Kings and queens still reigned and made decisions over their countries. But America was a newborn nation, a place where class or birthright had never mattered as much as it did in Great Britain. The brutal struggles of the early days of colonization had birthed a nation of people whose focus had been more on survival than convention. Even the Church, being almost completely Protestant compared to the mostly Catholic or Anglican Europeans, was more liberal in America.

The Articles of Confederation

Starting shortly after the American Revolution, America was governed under the Articles of Confederation. The states were governed by a Congress, consisting of representatives from each state, and all decisions were put to a vote by the states. At least nine of the thirteen states had to agree in order for any changes to be made. This concept attempted to unify the various states, which were based on the original Thirteen Colonies, but failed miserably.

On the surface, this may have seemed like a good idea. No single person had full control over the country; it was hoped that this would prevent the kind of tyranny that had often been seen in Europe under selfish, power-hungry monarchs. Unfortunately, the confederacy quickly disintegrated into a chaos of power-grabbing by the various states, all of which were vying for resources and arguing over their borders.

It quickly became evident that America needed a single, unifying leader who would be able to bring the states together and lead them forward into a new era of peace. America had fought too hard for its independence to lose itself in homeland squabbles. And who better to lead the newly-fledged country than the man who had fought so hard to establish it?

The Unanimous Election

The Constitutional Convention was held in Philadelphia in 1787 where the Constitution of the United States was drawn up. This vital document laid the foundation upon which the government would be built, and while it was amended over the following centuries, it remains the bedrock of American law. At the convention, it was also decided that a president would have to be chosen. Apparently, it was obvious to the Electoral College that there was only one man who would be fit for that role. George Washington had proven himself countless times in battle, and he was an educated man who also happened to come from a fairly aristocratic British family, which would help to gain respect from Great Britain itself. His will for independence and a determination to establish a new and fairer government than the tyrannical monarchies of the Old World was, however, very much American. In early 1789, the Electoral College—consisting of delegates from the different states—cast their votes. Washington was unanimously elected, the only U.S. president ever to receive that honor.

There was just one problem. Washington didn't want to be president. At fifty-seven, having weathered two long wars and seeing more bloodshed than any man was meant to, he wanted nothing but peace. His sole desire was to retire to his beautiful farm at Mount Vernon where he could watch over peaceful fields and gaze upon a country view, enjoying the independence and tranquility that he had fought so hard to bring to his nation. It must have seemed to him that he had done enough. Yet the nation's need for leadership was insatiable, and their voices were adamant: they wanted Washington and nobody else. Reluctantly, he agreed, and he was inaugurated in April 1789 at New York City, which was then the capital of America.

The First Presidency

For this president, there was no precedent. Not only was he the first president of America, but he was also one of the first presidents anywhere; democracy was in its infancy, and there was no model for what Washington was about to do. The concept of the leader being a civil servant as opposed to a ruling monarch was a new one. In Washington's own words, "I walk on untrodden ground."

The politics of the new America were indeed groundbreaking. One defining characteristic of Washington's presidency was his determination to prove that he was an unselfish leader whose purpose was to help and care for the people, not to exploit them; unlike the kings and queens of the Old World, who amassed as much wealth as they could and tended toward filling their own coffers before they thought of filling the stomachs of their people, Washington wouldn't even accept his own presidential salary at first. He wanted to set a standard for other presidents to follow, a standard of unselfishness and dedication. During his first term, he was able to stabilize this new nation, tackling the problem of the national debt it had been left with by the Revolution and succeeding in improving its fledgling finances.

When the presidential elections of 1792 came around again, Washington was once again unanimously elected. Like the first time, Washington did his best to resist, but the people refused to hear him—they needed him, and their decision was final. Eventually, he agreed to serve a second term, and it was a good thing. Britain and France were about to go to war once again, and this left America in a difficult position. Technically it was allied with France, but Washington knew that his little nation was by no means ready to mess with international affairs; they had beaten the British once, but the war had left the nation depleted of resources. The looming giant of the British Empire was also not far away; Canada, right on the border of America, was still a British colony. Wisely, in 1793, Washington decided to maintain a position of neutrality. This broke the terms of his treaty with France, but it proved to be a good decision. America did not get involved in the messy French Revolutionary Wars, which would last for decades.

Despite his best efforts, however, Washington would have to be involved in fighting one last time. When Washington's administration agreed to place a tax on spirits in 1791, it eventually sparked a violent revolt known as the Whiskey Rebellion. The old general himself led a federal militia into Pennsylvania to put down the rebellion; it was quickly and forcefully crushed, and the message was abundantly clear. As much as Washington spoke of peace, the law would be enforced no matter the cost.

A Sad Goodbye

The Congress Hall in Philadelphia was packed with people as George Washington took his place before his people one last time. He gazed out over the assembled multitudes with a mixture of love and relief. For eight years, he had served as their president, and he had done his best to bring them happiness and safety. Now, he was going to address them for the last time.

"Friends and Citizens," he began. "The period for a new election of a citizen to administer the executive government of the United States being not far distant…"

Washington went on to deliver his Farewell Address, a document that has remained famous to this day. It is looked upon as a symbol of what American politics stand for and has long since been used as the standard against which other presidents are measured. The address spent quite some time defending Washington's decision not to serve a third term regardless of how much his people wanted him to—an act of unselfishness and humility that would be intensely rare in the centuries of presidencies to come. In his address, Washington humbly apologized for any mistakes he might unintentionally have made during his presidency. He also pardoned the rebels who had been involved in the Whiskey Rebellion and stepped down from the stand ready to partake in "the benign influence of good laws under a free government, the ever-favorite object of my heart, and the happy reward, as I trust, of our mutual cares, labors, and dangers."

For the next two years, Washington would do just that. He died peacefully on his beloved farm in 1799.

Chapter 8 – Restless Times

After George Washington stepped down in 1797, John Adams was elected president. He had served as Washington's vice president and seemed an able leader, but it wouldn't be long before his presidency was plagued with violence.

The XYZ Affair

Even before Washington's presidency ended, the French had a bone to pick with the United States. Ever since the U.S. had signed Jay's Treaty with Great Britain—which effectively resolved many of the long-standing conflicts that had been plaguing the two nations—the French were bitter and resentful. They had fought on the American side during the Revolution, and they felt that it was extremely unfair that America now sided with Britain, which was France's enemy. The French went as far as seizing American merchant ships.

In a bid to reestablish some kind of diplomatic relations with France, John Adams sent three American diplomats to Paris to meet with the foreign minister of France. At first, the minister refused to see the Americans at all; after much negotiation, he finally agreed to see them but only if they paid him a bribe and agreed to lend money to France. Horrified, the Americans refused. In 1798, Congress rescinded the Treaty of Alliance, and the nations were just a declaration away from open war.

The Quasi-War

While Adams was forced to prepare for war—forming the Department of the Navy and building American warships for the first time—he was wise enough not to declare war openly. Something, however, would have to be done about French attacks on American merchant vessels. American warships were given permission to attack French ships, and several were sent to guard the waters near Long Island.

One of these was the beautiful USS *Constellation*. Named after the then-fifteen stars on the United States flag, the *Constellation* was an elegant frigate, rigged with huge sails and bearing 38 massive guns. She was commanded by Captain Thomas Truxtun and became one of the most successful warships of the Navy during that time, with her first victory being on a wintry day when the French warship *L'Insurgente* came across her patrolling the West Indies on February 9th, 1799. The peaceful waters of the Caribbean boiled and frothed as gunfire exploded above them; splinters crashed into the water, blood curling in the blue ocean, foaming pink on the edges of the tossing waves. *L'Insurgente* managed to get close enough to make an attempt to board the *Constellation*, but Truxtun succeeded in skillfully maneuvering his ship away and returning fire. Outgunned, *L'Insurgente* was forced to surrender.

About a year later, the *Constellation* would also fight one of the last battles of the Quasi-War. On February 1st, 1800, she came across *La Vengeance*. Despite the fact that the French warship had twelve more guns than the *Constellation*, the Americans fired on the French so relentlessly that *La Vengeance* eventually had to flee.

While the United States lost thousands of merchant vessels during the Quasi-War, it was also able to gain 85 French warships. Things were looking good for the U.S. when negotiators finally managed to bring a peaceful resolution to a war that never was declared. The Treaty of Mortefontaine was signed on September 30th, 1800.

Thomas Jefferson as President

Adams served long enough to see the Quasi-War end. Thomas Jefferson, the writer of the Declaration of Independence, was inaugurated in 1801 and served two fairly peaceful terms. He oversaw an era of invention and exploration, as well as the end of America's role in the horrific Middle Passage that had caused so much pain, death, and suffering to African slaves being shipped over the Atlantic. Slavery was still very much a part of American life, but the trade with Africa had ended at last.

During Jefferson's second term, Robert Fulton invented the steamboat. Further advancing a spirit of invention and discovery, Jefferson also commissioned the Lewis and Clark Expedition, which was the first expedition to cross all the way to the western side of the United States. Added to this, he negotiated the Louisiana Purchase, in which the United States paid the equivalent of fifteen million dollars today for the French territory of Louisiana, allowing the U.S. access to the valuable port of New Orleans and the Mississippi River. His successful presidency ended in 1809, and James Madison, the architect of the Constitution, was elected in his place.

The War of 1812

Madison had been president for three years, and America was just getting used to real peace when chaos threatened in Europe once more.

While Adams and Washington—both of the Federalist Party—had worked hard to improve relations with the British, the next two presidents were Democratic-Republicans, who were against working with Britain and wanted to improve an alliance with France instead. With the Democratic-Republicans in office, the relationship with Britain worsened steadily over the years. Trade was injured by struggling relations with both Britain and France, and to make matters worse, the two European powers were squabbling for trading rights with America. American merchants were restless for a resolution so that they could continue to ship their goods to Europe; American farmers were more restless still as they had nowhere to sell their produce. Added to this was the British impressment of sailors, with thousands of American sailors being effectively kidnapped for service in the British navy. Finally, in 1812, Madison signed a declaration of war against Great Britain. The British and Americans were at each other's throats once again.

Much of the war was fought on the Canadian border as the United States made three attempts to invade their British-held neighbor. None of these were successful; instead, the British managed to ally with Native Americans in the northwestern parts of America, and there were several battles fought and lost between U.S. forces and the Brits with their Indian allies. Chaos reigned for more than two years, costing thousands of lives on both sides before a peace treaty was finally signed in Europe on Christmas Eve, 1814.

The trouble was that nobody in America knew that a treaty had been signed. There was no telephone or Internet in those days; the only way to communicate was by letter or messenger, which took about a month to cross over from Europe to America. Thus, the most decisive battle of the War of 1812 was fought after the war itself had ended. The Battle of New Orleans on January 8th, 1815, saw a fierce American victory when Major General Andrew Jackson, who had been a prisoner of the British during the Revolutionary War, formed an impenetrable line of fire that forced the British back. Despite the fact that the war itself ended in more or less a stalemate, the Battle of New Orleans led the American psyche to consider the war a victory.

Chapter 9 – Horrors for the Natives

The sound of thousands of feet shuffling along the dirt echoed across the landscape. The mass of men, women, and children extended down the trail as far as the eye could see, enveloped in a cloud of dust, disease, and dismay. The barren landscape seemed incapable of yielding so much as a wildflower, let alone any real sustenance, and even if it had, there was no opportunity to stop for hunting or gathering. There was just marching and more marching—day in and day out, for more than a thousand miles, all of it on foot.

The only horses belonged to the white men. They sat upon their steeds with their guns, gesturing angrily with their weapons if any of their unhappy charges dared to do so much as slow down. The wisest thing was simply to lower one's head, stare down at one's feet, and shuffle forward. And with every step, home—a place of lands and farms, with towns and friendships, churches and schools—was left farther and farther behind.

The Cherokee women clutched their children as close as they could as if the strength of their love could somehow shield them from the hardships that lay before them. So many of them had died already. Crammed together in a stifling herd, like so many cattle, the over

16,500 Cherokees were used to hygienic lifestyles. The kids had been in missionary schools. The people had lived in well-built homes, worked all day in fresh air. They had had their own written language. They'd printed newspapers and written songs. The nation had been governed by an organized, elected administration of their own people. All of it had been a bid to fit in, a bid to become like the white men so that they wouldn't be destroyed the way that their neighbors had been. But none of that remained now; all there was now was marching, sometimes in manacles, and trying to survive.

The sounds of coughing filled the defeated ranks as they headed farther away from their ancestral territories in Georgia, Alabama, North Carolina, and Tennessee. Like the Chickasaw, Choctaw, and Creek nations, the Cherokee had been living there for generations upon generations. Ever since the settlers first came, some had been living peacefully among them, while others fought back, often resulting in bloody massacres where both white men and natives committed the most heinous crimes of mass murder and relentless cruelty. But now the greed of the white Americans had won. The Cherokees, like the others, were being forcibly relocated—forced at gunpoint to march to some place called "Indian country." At this point, with children dying all around them from all manner of diseases, diseases that spread like wildfire in their cramped and dirty ranks, many of them had lost any hope of ever seeing this Indian country. Others wondered if it existed at all.

These sad thoughts were not unfounded. By the time they reached Indian country—a part of modern-day Oklahoma—one-quarter of the Cherokee were dead. They had died as a result of disease and starvation as they were driven ruthlessly away from their homes. The 1,200 miles that they had walked became known as the Trail of Tears, a road of anguish and suffering that they would never forget.

Jackson as President

It all began on March 4th, 1829, when Andrew Jackson was inaugurated as president of the United States. This was an understandable move considering that the fledgling democracy limited voting only to white men—no Native Americans, slaves, or women were allowed to vote. If they had any say, Jackson would have been the last man ever allowed to come near the newly-built White House (the old President's House was burned down by the British in 1814).

To those who were allowed to vote, Jackson was a hero. He had been the one to beat the British at the Battle of New Orleans. It was his line of stakes and rifles—the "Jackson Line"—that had held back the mighty force of redcoats and eventually drove them into the wasteland and wilderness. He had proven himself to be tough, tenacious, determined, and ready to do anything needed to protect the interests of those whom he saw as his responsibility.

The trouble was that he had never seen Native Americans as the same kind of human as the other citizens of the United States. Prior to the War of 1812, Jackson's role in the army had mostly consisted of fighting Native Americans. He had spent much time subduing the Creek Nation, eventually seizing 22 million acres of their land and giving them to white farmers instead. This made him hugely popular with the farmers, who expected him to give them even more land once he was president—and they were not disappointed.

The Indian Removal Act

Starting in the early 1830s, Jackson pushed for Native Americans to be forced out of their desirable and fertile lands in the South and driven northwest to barren prairies that nobody really wanted. The discovery of gold in Georgia only made matters worse. Even before any legislation was passed, farmers who had lived peacefully alongside their Native American counterparts started to view their neighbors with suspicion. Some Native Americans made matters worse for themselves by lashing out, often kidnapping white children to be used as pawns in later negotiations with the whites; this only spread the rumors that these "Injuns" were savages, evil, and somehow less than human.

On a more national scale, Jackson was doing everything in his power to seize as much land as possible from the Native Americans. Even before his presidency, he had helped to negotiate a series of treaties that convinced Native Americans to sign over their southern and eastern lands for uncharted territory somewhere in the West. Despite the fact that the natives probably knew the Western lands would be infertile and poor compared to the lands they already owned, many of them agreed, knowing they had little choice. War with the white man would invite disaster; better, then, to go away into the West and hope that they wouldn't be bothered there.

Before he even took the presidency, Jackson had been persecuting Native Americans ruthlessly, being heavily involved in the First Seminole War during the 1810s. In 1830, things got far worse for the Native Americans when Jackson succeeded in passing the Indian Removal Act. This act allowed Jackson to negotiate treaties with the Native Americans that would force them to give up their eastern lands and migrate west of the Mississippi. Arguing that the Native Americans weren't educated enough to make their own decisions, Jackson persuaded Congress that removal would be a good thing for them. The act was supposed to allow only for peaceful and voluntary relocation; those natives that refused to give up their lands were supposed to be granted citizenship of the state where they were currently residing. But with a president so strongly against the natives, this was never going to happen. The Choctaws, signing a treaty in 1830, were the first to leave for their western lands, hoping for a better life there. Some stayed behind but were so badly harassed and mistreated by their white neighbors that they eventually sold their farms and left.

The Cherokee were not so easily fooled. At first, when about 500 Cherokee members, known as the Treaty Party, signed the Treaty of New Echota in 1835, it looked as though they would follow the example of the Choctaws and simply leave. The treaty agreed to hand over the eastern Cherokee lands in exchange for a cash payment, new lands in the West, and some other aid in moving.

However, most of the Cherokee, including the tribal leadership, had not agreed to the treaty. This became evident when Chief John Ross put together a petition against the treaty. Signed by 16,000 Cherokee, this petition should have been more than enough to put a stop to the Treaty of New Echota, but it was flatly ignored.

The Trail of Tears

In 1836, the Creek Nation suffered a horrible fate that served as a warning for the Cherokees. The Creeks had been at war with white Americans for decades—in fact, Jackson himself had led 2,500 men to fight against the Creeks in 1813 and 1814. He even ordered General John Coffee to attack a village which ended in the massacre of 186 Creek warriors, including numerous women and children. The butchering had been so terrible that Creek mothers fell to killing their own babies to avoid letting them die brutally at the hands of the Americans.

While the war had ended, the Americans were still not letting the Creeks keep their lands. In 1836, 15,000 Creeks were forcibly marched from their homes in Alabama to Indian country in Oklahoma. Only 11,500 actually made it there.

A similar fate awaited the Cherokees. As much as they kicked back against the treaty, with even the Supreme Court ruling the Cherokee tribe as a sovereign nation, which technically should have given them legal protection against any kind of forced removal, Jackson ignored his own laws and ordered them to be marched to Indian country in 1838. Over 16,500 Cherokees left Georgia; 4,000 of them perished along the way.

The Seminole Wars

The Seminoles, a tribe living in Florida, had long been clashing with white Americans as well. Jackson himself had been sent to subdue them shortly after the War of 1812; he had succeeded in forcing them into a reservation in central Florida, kicked the Spanish out of the state, and claimed it as a United States territory. Despite all this, white settlers continued to clamor for more and more land in their new state.

After the Indian Removal Act was passed, another attempt was made to move the Seminole, this time in a bid to force them out of Florida entirely and relocate them to Oklahoma like the Creeks and Cherokees. A council of Seminole chiefs agreed to journey to the new lands and decide whether or not they were fit for habitation by their tribes. While the chiefs signed the Treaty of Payne's Landing, agreeing to move their tribes, they later told their tribes that they had been forced to sign it. On their return to Florida, they announced that they were not going to move a single family.

Regardless of this, the treaty was ratified, and the Seminole prepared for war. Led by their chief, Osceola, they put up the most strenuous resistance of any Native American tribe at the time. From 1835 to 1842, they fought the white Americans tooth and nail, determined to cling onto the lands where they had been living since their legends could remember. They were eventually defeated, with only a handful left living on their little reservation in Florida, but their defeat came at a high price to the Americans: about 1,600 of their soldiers died in the fighting.

At last, by the early 1840s, the majority of Native Americans had been forced into Indian country. Here they hoped they were going to be left alone in peace and allowed to hold onto their new lands for the rest of their lives. But these hopes were short-lived. The hunger for American expansion knew no limits. The call of the frontier would not be ignored.

Chapter 10 – Awakening

Illustration IV: San Francisco Harbor near the height of the Gold Rush

Charles G. Finney's words echoed around the field. An assembly of thousands of faces stared up at him, their expressions rapt, their eyes locked on him as he stood on a stump and rang out the words of one of his most famous sermons.

His eyes shone as he preached. "And in reference to the present, the obvious truth is that if our conscience fully approves of our state, and we are conscious of having acted according to the best light we have, it contradicts all our just ideas of God to suppose that he condemns us." He laughed, throwing open his arms, reveling in the wide-eyed wonder of the people listening. Most of them had grown up learning the Protestant doctrine; they had always been taught that there was no way to be sure of salvation. But Finney believed that there was a deeper love in God that would allow His children to be confident in their eternity. "He is a father," he went on, "and He cannot but smile on His obedient and trusting children."

His stirring words raised shouts of "Amen!" from the crowd. All around him, other preachers' rousing words echoed around the camp meeting, their clenched fists brandished in the air, their audiences shouting out, caught up in the joy of the moment. The Second Great Awakening may have begun in c. 1790, but it was due to preachers like Finney that the movement gained any traction.

A Religious Revival

Following the Great Awakening of the 1730s through the 1750s in Great Britain and the Thirteen Colonies, the Second Great Awakening was another wave of revival that swept through the United States, borne forward by unlikely preachers. In that era, ministers and church leaders were usually university educated. Their academics were almost as rigorous as those of lawyers or doctors; once qualified, they easily fell into the trap of considering themselves loftier than the people of their flock. But the Second Great Awakening saw a new idea enter the hearts of the people: the thought that God could use anyone, no matter how lowly, no matter how uneducated. That even ordinary people could change the world.

This awakening followed upon the heels of a nation that was bolstered by its recent victories in the wars it had been fighting. From the Revolution through the War of 1812 and the Seminole Wars, the non-native citizens of the United States had yet to suffer a major defeat. Their national identity was growing ever stronger; the "Star-Spangled Banner" was on the lips of every citizen. It was a time of peace and prosperity. With most of their enemies defeated, the Americans could turn their thoughts to things other than survival.

The Second Great Awakening would also give birth to two new ideas that would soon shape the history of America: feminism and abolitionism. But first, the nation would be distracted by the discovery of gold.

The Discovery at Sutter's Mill

When James Wilson Marshall first saw the little metallic glimmer in the shallows of the river, he didn't think much of it. His mind was occupied with his work. A carpenter, Marshall was busy building a waterwheel for his client, John Sutter. Turning away from the river, he returned his attention to the wood and nails that he was working with.

But something about that little flash he'd seen in the water was niggling at him. After a few minutes' work, he put down his hammer and went to investigate. Stepping cautiously into the shallows of the American River, he felt the cold water splashing over his feet, freezing his toes with its wintry January bite. He searched the pebbles. Had his eyes deceived him?

Then he saw it. Something bright, wedged between the pebbles. Marshall's heart was pounding. He slowly leaned closer, searching the shallow water, his mouth dry. There it was—a tiny nugget that shone with a warm glow where the sunlight struck it. Marshall reached into the cold water and pinched the lump of metal between his fingertips then drew it out into the air. It lay on his trembling palm, glowing, and Marshall knew at once that it was gold.

The California Gold Rush

Marshall's discovery of gold on January 24th, 1848 in the American River was at first met with suspicion. Other Americans simply couldn't believe that California really held untold wealth. The territory had just been part of the subject of war between America and Mexico; its population numbered just over 6,000 *Californios—*

people primarily of Spanish American descent—150,000 Native Americans and only 800 white Americans. There were a few little farms and a few little towns. San Francisco itself was little more than a speck on the map. Surely, of all the places where gold could be, California wasn't it.

Then everything changed a few weeks later when Sam Brannan, a storekeeper in San Francisco, brought a vial of glittering gold into the streets and marched around the town, displaying it for all to see. America was convinced. There was gold in California after all, and suddenly, every American wanted a piece of it.

The California Gold Rush would start in earnest in 1849 and continue into the early 1850s, peaking in 1852. Seized by "gold fever," thousands of American men left their homes, lives, and families behind to make their way to the mines. 75% of San Franciscan men left the city. For the first time, women were forced to become fully independent, running farms and business single-handedly while they raised their kids and cared for their homes. Californians weren't the only ones headed for the frontier—people traveled from as far away as Peru, Hawaii, other parts of the United States, and even China to get their share of the gold.

At first, gold was easy pickings; getting it was as simple as picking it up off the dirt. Later, it had to be panned from the river, and later still, as the supply of gold dwindled in the face of the insatiable thirst for wealth, it had to be obtained by hydraulic mining. Thousands of men had mortgaged their homes or spent everything they had to get to California, and they were desperate to get their investment back. This resulted in thousands of Native Americans being pushed out of their territory.

Lasting Legacy of the Gold Rush

The California Gold Rush's impact on the state and the country remains to this day. Hundreds of small mining towns popped up throughout the state, many of them now large cities. The Gold Rush also expedited California's admittance as the 31st state in 1850.

California's economy boomed, as did its population; with over 300,000 Americans moving into the state, the Gold Rush became known as the largest mass migration in American history.

At its peak, the Gold Rush yielded more than $80 million in gold in a single year. After 1852, however, it slowly started to decline until it reached about $45 million in 1857 and remained more or less stable after that. Hydraulic mining, which yielded plenty of gold but wrought havoc on the landscape, was banned in 1884.

Chapter 11 – Civil War

As the Gold Rush brought wealth to thousands and ruin to many more, the United States found itself embroiled in a controversy. California's application to become a state had caused a significant stir in Congress. No one could deny that Californian land was valuable, but the new state brought with it a new question: was it to be a slave or free state?

During that period, the United States was already divided over the issue of slavery. The Second Great Awakening had brought with it a new wave of abolitionism, with many Americans converting to a form of Christianity that renounced the slave trade as being against the will of God. The Northern states, in particular, were mostly free, meaning that slaves could not be kept in them at all. The Southern states, however, relied heavily on the slave trade, both as an economy in itself and for labor to work on lucrative tobacco, cotton, and sugarcane plantations.

Before the admission of California, the states were fairly evenly divided: about half were free states and the other half slave states. The admission of California, Oregon, New Mexico, and Utah, however, was likely to tip the balance in the direction of more free states than slave. This caused widespread anger and even panic among the Southern states, who feared they would lose their power. War came perilously close to breaking out until Henry Clay came up with the Compromise of 1850, which settled the Southern states down but still allowed California to be admitted as a free state.

Chaos on the Frontier

While hundreds of Americans were working their way across the continent, staking their claims in new lands and pushing the border of the country ever outward, the clash between anti- and pro-slavery groups continued to grow. Pioneers moving into the territory of Kansas were particularly violent. The Kansas-Nebraska Act essentially allowed Kansas to decide whether to allow slavery or not, a decision that proved wildly unpopular with strongly convicted Northerners who didn't want their new lands tainted by the slave trade, which they viewed as sinful and criminal. Fights broke out often between anti- and pro-slavery groups, who generally migrated from Missouri, while the anti-slavery parties often came from New England. The violence, known today as "Bleeding Kansas," cost many lives in a variety of bloody massacres.

Bleeding Kansas was just a foreshadow of things to come. The balance of power had undeniably shifted, despite the best efforts of the Southern states; slavery was no longer as fashionable as it had once been, and the suffering of the enslaved blacks was starting to enrage more and more Americans. And in 1861, this disagreement would erupt into full-scale civil war.

The Start of the War

The fate of the nation hinged on the 1860 presidential election. The nation was profoundly divided, with the Democratic party split into a Northern and a Southern faction; the Northern Democrats were fairly neutral on the issue of slavery, while the Southerners were distinctly pro-slavery. The Republican Party, on the other hand, led by Abraham Lincoln, was radically anti-slavery.

When Lincoln won the election, the South felt that this was a terrible injustice. Lincoln had not won any of the Southern states; they had simply been outnumbered and overwhelmed by votes from the more numerous Northern states. Tired of the deep divide between North and South, a group of seven Southern states—Mississippi, Alabama, Texas, Louisiana, Georgia, South Carolina, and Florida—seceded from the United States and renamed themselves the Confederate States of America. They would later be joined by Tennessee, North Carolina, Virginia, and Arkansas.

With the country utterly divided, the Northern states (still known as the United States) refused to recognize the secession. Lincoln and his administration feared that allowing this secession would ultimately divide the United States into a chaotic mass of small countries, not unlike Europe, which had been embroiled in war for centuries. On April 12th, 1861, a Confederate army captured Fort Sumter in Charleston Bay, and the first shots were fired. The Civil War was under way.

Growing Battles

The Civil War would see the largest battles that the United States had ever engaged in. As the Confederate army under Robert E. Lee clashed repeatedly with the Union army commanded by General George G. Meade, the scope of the battles only grew larger and larger. Lincoln's original tactic had been to limit the war as much as possible, simply attempting to subdue what he viewed as a rebellion in the South. However, as the war went on, the cost of the fighting grew, with thousands of human lives being poured into the struggle regarding the freedom of African Americans. Many thousands of these lives belonged to free African Americans from the North, drawn by Lincoln's issue of the Emancipation Proclamation which declared all slaves in the rebel states to be legally free, even though their masters refused to give them up.

The Battle of Gettysburg, taking place on July 1st to July 3rd, 1863, was the turning point of the Civil War. Prior to Gettysburg, Lee had enjoyed multiple victories over the Union. At this fight, however, it was Meade who would win the day—at a horrific cost. There were over 50,000 casualties, including over 7,000 dead, 33,000 wounded, and nearly 11,000 missing. The death toll was so terrible that Lincoln was moved to declare total war on the South, determined to wipe out its entire slave culture for good.

In 1864, Ulysses S. Grant became the leading Union general in the Virginian theater, where the fighting was the most heated. Between Grant, William T. Sherman, and other Union generals, the intense fighting was finally able to push the Confederates back. Grant was the one who was able to corner Lee and force him to surrender on April 9th, 1865.

The Assassination of Abraham Lincoln

Lincoln was only able to enjoy the taste of victory for a sparse five days. On April 14th, 1865, actor and Confederate supporter John Wilkes Booth shot Lincoln in the back of the head while he was peacefully watching a play with his wife and guests. Booth escaped into the night, leading to a nationwide manhunt that ended twelve days later when he was shot and killed.

It was too late for Lincoln, however. He was pronounced dead the next morning on April 15th. Yet his dream was far from dead; the war officially ended a few weeks later on May 9th, 1865, when the last stragglers of the Confederate Army surrendered. Slavery was over, but so were the lives of 620,000 soldiers. To this day, that number is almost half the total amount of American soldiers that have ever died in combat throughout history. Worse, many of these soldiers were fighting against friends and family; no longer were they just fighting a nameless foe but people they knew. The profound rift caused by the war would be as heartbreaking as it was violent.

Freedom had definitely been earned at the dearest cost. Now, it was time to rebuild an entire nation.

Chapter 12 – Seeking for Peace

The task that fell to the next American president would not be an easy one. With Abraham Lincoln dead and the nation in tatters after a decimating civil war, someone was going to have to take the reins and rebuild the country almost from its foundations. Four million African Americans had been freed from slavery; now, they had to be integrated into the rest of society somehow, while the South's economy and infrastructure had to be rebuilt. The task fell to Andrew Johnson, Lincoln's vice president. He had narrowly escaped assassination himself as Booth's co-conspirator, who had been given the task to kill Johnson that night, had elected to drink himself into a stupor instead.

It seemed that Johnson had run out of luck though. Despite the fact that he made numerous achievements in his presidency—including the Alaska Purchase and the 13th Amendment which saw slavery finally abolished in December 1865—Johnson proved unpopular with radical Republicans and many of the former Union states when he effectively allowed the Southern states to govern themselves whichever way they liked, apart from having to adhere to the abolition of slavery. The South responded by passing "black codes" which limited the behavior and freedom of African Americans to such an extent that many Republicans in Congress viewed the codes as little better than slavery.

In 1868, Ulysses S. Grant, the general whose efforts had hugely contributed to the Union victory, was elected president. He and Johnson hated each other so much that Johnson refused to even attend Grant's inauguration, but to most of the U.S., Grant was a hero; it was thought that he would be less likely to cast the hard-won victory of the Union to the winds. He gathered the reins well, placing far more emphasis on the Reconstruction Era than Johnson had.

Opposition to a Rebuilt Nation

In 1870, blacks were given suffrage for the first time in the 15th Amendment. All males, regardless of race, were now allowed to vote. African Americans could now be elected to state governments and even to Congress, and those who had been slaves less than ten years earlier found themselves suddenly possessing the same rights as their white counterparts (although laws were put into place to guarantee these rights would be hard, if impossible, to obtain).

This incensed many white Southerners, some of whom turned to violence against proponents of Reconstruction. White supremacy was not forgotten—instead, it was a cause for which many Southerners were still prepared to fight. The most radical of these formed the strange and severely creepy Ku Klux Klan.

Dressed in robes to disguise their identity so that all that was visible of the wearer was a glimpse of his eyes, members of the Ku Klux Klan existed to sow terror among minorities and those who supported their cause and advance white supremacy in the Southern states once more. Formed almost immediately after the Civil War ended, the Klan committed hundreds of acts of violence against newly-emancipated African Americans and their allies. Their robes provided them with enough anonymity that they felt invincible, and they acted accordingly, murdering and destroying wherever they went. They were very active until the 1870s which is when their activities trailed off, although other iterations of the Klan have taken place throughout the years. Legislation was passed against the Klan which did help suppress the group, but the damage was already done to African Americans, especially when it came to voting and politics.

The interest in Reconstruction began to wane through the mid-1870s as it became evident that the South was functioning once more with African Americans integrated into their new roles, although they still weren't being treated fairly. In 1874, Democrats once again rose to power, gaining control over the House of Representatives. The Civil War seemed to be largely left behind less than ten years after it had ended.

The Wild West

Now that peace had befallen the nation once more, Americans started to turn their focus to expansionism again. The Western frontier was still largely unexplored, and it was here that one of the most dramatic eras of United States history began: that of the legendary Wild West.

The Old West era extended from the Civil War to about 1895— thirty years that would become the American era most immortalized in culture. The names of the famous men and women of that era echo throughout the centuries with irresistible familiarity: Billy the Kid, Jesse James, Calamity Jane, Chief Sitting Bull, Annie Oakley, Wild Bill Hickok. The West was sparsely populated and lawless; while it was mostly inhabited by peaceful cattle ranchers, its open lands provided plenty of space for outlaws to hide, and the little towns held banks for robbing and saloons for entertainment. To tell all of the stories of the Old West would take dozens of books, but the reality of this romanticized era was all too tragic.

America had barely finished its Civil War when it began a long and bloody struggle with the Plains Indians. The Native Americans that had relocated to the West now found themselves surrounded by whites whose hunger for new land had still not been satisfied, and to make matters worse, the West was already inhabited by tribes who had been living there for hundreds of years. The Plains Indians were some of the last tribes left living on their ancestral lands, and they'd seen how attempts at peaceful negotiations with the settlers had ended for other Native American tribes. They were determined to go to war.

To make matters worse, these tribes' livelihoods depended largely on the huge herds of bison that roamed the plains. Unfortunately, bison were a lucrative target for the new settlers; they were killed by the thousands, decimating the population, endangering the species, and stripping the Native Americans of their most important food source.

The Plains Indian tribes—which included the Apache, Sioux, and Cheyenne, among others—were determined not to suffer the same fate that their Southern neighbors had during the Trail of Tears. They fought back, with bloody consequences.

The Wounded Knee Massacre

Chief Spotted Elk knew that he was alone.

Crazy Horse had been dead for over thirteen years. Sitting Bull's blood was still warm on the earth, but he, too, was gone. It was just Spotted Elk now as he led his band of Lakota natives toward the Pine Ridge Reservation. As much as the Native Americans had been struggling against having to go to the reservations, they knew that they had no choice anymore. The very place that they had tried so hard to avoid had become their only safe refuge.

Spotted Elk could only hope that the Ghost Dances would work. Native American religions were as complex as they were dynamic, a moving, growing thing that had assimilated the coming of the white man and produced the Ghost Dance, which they believed would set them free from their oppressors. If they could just perform the Ghost Dance over and over, then their gods would avenge them. A new earth could be recreated—one where the ships never came, where the Native Americans could continue to live with free rein on the continent where their culture had been born.

But the Ghost Dances did nothing except anger and frighten the U.S. Army. Believing that these were war dances, they had kept a close eye on the Ghost Dancers ever since the movement began, and Spotted Elk's little troop would be no exception. On December 28th, as the Lakota were encamped on the banks of Wounded Knee Creek, they found themselves surrounded by the U.S. 7th Cavalry. Its commander, Colonel James Forsyth, told them that they were only there to escort the Lakota to Pine Ridge. But the Hotchkiss guns surrounding the perimeter—machine guns capable of firing up to 500 rounds per minute—told a different story.

Their fears were realized when the U.S. soldiers ordered them to surrender their weapons the next day. Tension filled the camp as some of the Lakota tightened their grips on tomahawks and rifles, wary of the soldiers' motives. Then, the medicine man, Yellow Bird, raised his voice in a thin, droning melody that signaled the start of the Ghost Dance. Seizing the hands of the two people nearest him, he started the shuffling dance. The others hurried to link arms, and before the soldiers knew what was happening, a giant circle of Lakota was moving around and around in the monotony that allowed them to keep their dance going for hours. The Ghost Dance had begun.

The atmosphere was leaden, drawn out with fear on both sides. Nervous shouts to stop echoed from some of the soldiers; however, the dance went on, relentless and unforgiving, the circle only pausing when some of the dancers started to grab handfuls of dirt and flung it into the air, filling the soldiers' vision with turning bodies and flying dust. Amid all this, one of the soldiers spotted Black Coyote, a young warrior, clutching his rifle. The soldier grabbed the rifle, demanding that Black Coyote give it up. He pulled it back, and suddenly, with a deafening crack in the muffled tension, the gun went off.

Panic reigned. Noise filled the camp as the Ghost Dance broke and Native Americans and soldiers alike were in all directions. There was shouting, some of the soldiers firing on Black Coyote, some of the Native Americans trying to stop them—and then the Hotchkiss guns spoke. Bullets poured into the camp, 2,000 a minute. Blood and screams filled the air, soaked into the dirt, and stained the face of U.S. history for all time. When the madness subsided, 300 Lakota were dead. 60 of them were women and children, innocents caught up in the chaos and killed in the crossfire.

The End of the Wars

The Wounded Knee Massacre brought an end to the decades of war between Native Americans and Americans of European descent. Hundreds of thousands of Native Americans had been killed since the Europeans first arrived; the native population dwindled from several million in the 15th century to only a few hundred thousand.

The wars had cost thousands of European American lives, too. The most famous defeat for the settlers, the Battle of the Little Bighorn in 1876, saw an entire regiment of soldiers under Colonel George Armstrong Custer wiped out by a band of Sioux and Cheyenne led by Sitting Bull and Crazy Horse. These were some of the last great Indian chiefs that attempted to rescue their tribes from the oncoming tide of Western expansionism, but after one of his own villages was destroyed by the U.S. Army in retaliation for the Little Bighorn chaos only days after that fateful battle, Crazy Horse surrendered in 1877. He died four months later, stabbed by a bayonet in prison at Fort Robinson.

By 1890, even Sitting Bull had all but given up: while there were still some battles between Plains Indians and the U.S. Army during the 1880s, Sitting Bull would lead no major fights. In fact, he didn't even participate in the Ghost Dances—although the reservation police mistakenly believed he did. In December 1890, they attempted to arrest him, shooting and killing him in the process, and prompting Spotted Elk's flight that eventually led to the last massacre at Wounded Knee. With the last great warrior chiefs gone, the Native Americans no longer put up much of a fight. The wars were over. The West was "won."

Chapter 13 – A Rising Power

By the close of the 19th century, there were 45 U.S. states. Thomas Edison had patented the light bulb, the National Geographic Society had been formed, the Constitution had celebrated its centennial, and Americans were even playing basketball. William McKinley was inaugurated as president in 1897, and, to a large extent, the nation was finally at peace with itself. While Native Americans had been confined to reservations, African Americans at least had been freed, although they still faced simmering racism.

With home affairs mostly under control, the United States began to emerge in foreign affairs as more than just a newly liberated colony. Now, the country was becoming a force to be reckoned with—and it would demonstrate just how powerful it had become with its first engagement in international war since the War of 1812.

The Spanish-American War

In 1898, while Florida had long since become a state, Spain still held several colonies in the Americas. One of these was Cuba, despite the best efforts of the Cubans themselves. Horrendously oppressed by their Spanish masters, Cubans had been fighting a bitter war ever since Carlos Manuel de Céspedes had rung the bell at the door of his sugar mill and told his slaves that they were free. His actions prompted the start of the Ten Years' War from 1868 to 1878, a dark struggle that had ended in hopeless defeat for the Cubans. They attempted to win their freedom again in the Little War of 1879 and were easily crushed by Spain.

For several years, things quietened down in Cuba, but the oppression did not end. Spaniards comprised only 2% of the Cuban population, yet they possessed most of the wealth on the island, leaving Cubans themselves struggling. In 1895, another effort to throw off Spanish shackles began, starting the Cuban War of Independence. The war resulted in nationwide chaos that eventually reached the capital, Havana. American citizens staying in Havana at the time feared for their lives, prompting the United States to send its latest pride and joy, the warship USS *Maine*, to lie at anchor in Havana Harbor as a silent warning to any who dared to drag American citizens into the mess.

The *Maine* was never supposed to go into action unless Americans were threatened. And she never did. Instead, on the evening of February 15th, 1898, she exploded. A fireball ripped out most of her hull, killing hundreds of crew members. The Spanish were widely blamed for the explosion, even though later evidence has strongly suggested that they were innocent and that the sinking of the *Maine* was a tragic accident. Outrage erupted in America, and together with the suffering of the Cuban people (who were, arguably, on their way to victory themselves), yellow journalism and the voice of the people forced President McKinley to declare war on Spain. The declaration was made on April 25th, 1898.

The Spanish-American War was short-lived. Where once America could never have hoped to hold a candle to the might of the Spanish Armada, now the United States had transformed into a military giant, and Spain—unprepared for war with the U.S. and weakened by decades of conflict with Cuba—never really stood a chance. By May 1st, the U.S. had won its first victory at Manila Bay in the Philippines, which was also tired of its status as a Spanish colony. In June, the U.S. Army reached Cuba, dispatching squadrons of men on both sea and land—including Theodore Roosevelt, then Lieutenant Colonel, and his Rough Riders. By July 1st, they were able to take the major city of Santiago de Cuba; in a bid to escape, the Spanish general tried to lead all of his men out of the city in warships on the morning of July 3rd, an attempt that failed dismally when the U.S. Navy was able to capture or sink all of the Spanish ships.

When Santiago de Cuba surrendered in mid-July, the war was practically over. The Spanish had known that they were defeated even before the war started; some fought with a fervor of desperation, but most of them were dragged down by lack of morale before they were defeated in battle. 90% of U.S. losses didn't even result from any form of Spanish resistance but was due to the infectious diseases that thrived in the tropical island of Cuba.

The Treaty of Paris left Spain stripped of several of its colonies. Cuba was granted its independence; Puerto Rico and Guam, on the other hand, were handed over to the United States. The U.S. had firmly established itself as a military juggernaut fully capable of handling itself in wars with Europe. Its new reputation would soon be tested. Within the next two decades, war would break out on a scale that had never been seen before.

Yankees Overseas

The boys were scared, and Ulysses Grant McAlexander knew it. Looking out over his line of white-faced soldiers, the colonel couldn't help but feel his heart go out to them. Just like him, they'd all been largely untested in international warfare—their nation had barely entered the Great War, and this would be the first time that American troops fought on foreign soil since the comparative cakewalk that had been the Spanish-American War twenty years ago.

Now, even McAlexander was starting to wonder if they were up to what they were about to face. He could hear the roar of the guns and voices as the German troops swarmed across the Marne, and he knew that the proximity of the sound meant that they'd already mowed right through the French 6th Army. It was really no surprise; Germany had been gaining ground in their recent offensive across France, despite the best efforts of the combined Allied army standing against them.

McAlexander felt the earth tremble beneath his feet in the trench. The deafening sound of shells was everywhere, sending great sprays of earth and blood flying into the air, scattering shrapnel and human flesh. He could see the Germans coming. They had crushed the French line, and on McAlexander's left and right, he could see his neighboring divisions buckling. Dug in on the riverbank, his 38th Infantry Regiment of the 3rd Division was ready to engage.

Gunfire erupted all around them. McAlexander shouted, cheering his men on as they dared to raise their helmets above the trenches and fire. Machine guns spoke loudly, rifles cracking and popping in the chaos. In the madness, McAlexander looked up to see that the lines on either side of his trench were buckling. The Germans were going to break through—they were going to make it and continue their offensive across France.

Through the smoke and dust of the fighting, McAlexander stared at his men. They were all looking at him, hearing the panicked orders to retreat from officers all around them. Only Colonel McAlexander had not yet told them to flee.

But something in him would not surrender. He took a deep breath. "*Nous resterons la*!" he shouted, loud and clear so that the Frenchmen around him would understand. "*Nous resterons la*! We shall remain here!"

Encouraged by the crystal-clear voice of their colonel, the men buckled down and returned fire courageously as the Germans threatened to overwhelm them. When their flanks became exposed as their allies fell away, left and right, McAlexander dragged them up, forming his division into a U-shape to protect its vulnerable sides. Despite the best that the Germans could throw at them, the 38th Infantry Regiment clung to its place on the edge of the Marne, eventually throwing their foes back when reinforcements rushed up at last to their aid. The Second Battle of the Marne proved instrumental in halting the German offensive, making room for the Allied counteroffensive that would eventually restore the balance of power in favor of the Allies, ultimately leading to their victory. And the heroes of the battle fought on July 15th, 1918, were the American 3rd Infantry Division. They became known as the "Rock of the Marne," and they proved to the rest of the world that the United States could stand shoulder to shoulder with the older nations when it came to military matters.

U.S. Involvement in World War I

American president Woodrow Wilson had never been interested in engaging in the war that was ripping Europe and Asia apart.

When WWI broke out on June 28th, 1914, Wilson had hurried to declare the United States' neutrality. Even though the Spanish-American War had been such a sweeping victory for the U.S., he knew that a world war was a different matter entirely. America was in its infancy compared to some of the ancient nations that were fighting in the Great War: Britain, Russia, France, and Germany had all been waging war on one another for longer than the United States had even existed. The fighting was mostly centered on Eurasia in any case. Let the war take care of itself.

But President Wilson's hopes that America's neutrality would keep it safe were unfounded. On May 7th, 1915, a British ocean liner became a victim of the deadly German U-boats. These stealthy submarines sent a torpedo spinning into the *Lusitania*'s hull, sinking it and killing more than a thousand people on board, including 128 American citizens. This, alongside an explosion on Black Tom Island in New Jersey orchestrated by German secret agents and a threatening telegram intercepted by British decoders in March 1917 that ordered Mexico to invade the United States, was enough to push Wilson over the edge. The United States declared war on April 6th, 1917.

Led by General John J. "Black Jack" Pershing, the American soldiers proved themselves quickly in battle. Among them was Major George S. Patton, someday to become one of the greatest (and yet most controversial) leaders of the Second World War. While just before WWI the entire American army numbered less than the French losses at the Battle of Verdun alone, by the end of the war, over two million U.S. soldiers had served on the Allied side. They contributed to the final offensive that eventually ended the Great War on November 11th, 1918.

With that, the United States had shown itself to be a formidable opponent in any war. Its military importance was unquestionable; its national pride and identity spurred on by success against its enemies. Yet this was but its baptism through fire. The United States still had a tremendous trial in international warfare to face in the century to come.

Chapter 14 – Progress

With a tenuous and flawed peace established all over the world, America found itself a changed nation.

More than a quarter of the young male population of the United States had served in the military during the First World War. Of that number, about 100,000 never came back. Those that did return to their homes and families when the war was over were not the same people that they had been when they left, fresh-faced and wide-eyed recruits riled up by propaganda and ready for some fighting. Now, they were broken, sometimes physically, often mentally. PTSD didn't have a name then; these men called their ailment shell shock or, often, nothing at all. Sometimes they just tried to carry on as if the death and devastation of the war didn't affect them, forcing them to drink or engage in similarly counterproductive measures in an attempt to cope with what medicine had not yet recognized as a legitimate mental disorder. This may have been part of what prompted Congress to pass the 18th Amendment, prohibiting the widespread consumption of alcohol that was causing social problems across the country. Prohibition eventually proved to be more trouble than it was worth, but it would endure until 1933.

What was more, with two million of their men overseas, the women of the United States had had to step into roles that society had long deemed unsuitable for them. Their newfound independence gave them a sense of power that was the last leg-up they needed to earn the right to vote. And when President Woodrow Wilson was suddenly and unexpectedly incapacitated, the First Lady would secretly do what American women had been doing ever since their men started to leave for the war: she would take over.

Women's Suffrage and Its Secret Leader

October 1st, 1919, was the last day that President Wilson would have full control over his own body. On the morning of October 2nd, he suffered a debilitating stroke that left almost half of his body paralyzed. Confined to his bed, he was constantly attended to by his personal physician, Dr. Cary T. Grayson, whose repeated warnings that Wilson's habit of overworking would lead to some medical disaster eventually, and his wife, First Lady Edith Wilson.

Edith was faced with a weighty responsibility. President Wilson could still speak and had a fair amount of mental clarity, but he was certainly incapable of working at the furious pace that had characterized his much-criticized presidency before the stroke. As much as Wilson's actions had been unpopular with a nation that had begged for war against Germany, he had won the Nobel Peace Prize in 1919 for his efforts in creating the League of Nations and negotiating the Treaty of Versailles—efforts that had contributed to the stroke that had almost killed him. Now, even though America may not have liked him, it needed him to complete the next two years to help navigate the world after the war. Edith's decision was simple: Woodrow would stay president. And she would help.

For the rest of President Wilson's term, Edith would secretly manage most of the affairs of the country. While she described herself as simply a "steward" who put all the important decisions to her husband, and while Woodrow himself likely still made many decisions, Edith was instrumental in running the country until Woodrow's term ended and he could finally be at rest in 1921.

For roughly a century, women had been campaigning for equal rights, demanding to be allowed to own property and to vote, which were only some of the rights that had been denied to them. However, diligent work over the decades by heroines such as Carrie Chapman Catt, Lucy Stone, Helen Blackburn, Susan B. Anthony, and Elizabeth Cady Stanton had secured voting rights for women in many of the states.

And progress was certainly being made. In the throes of the First World War, President Wilson himself had said that allowing women to vote was "vitally essential to the successful prosecution of the great war of humanity in which we are engaged."

The 19th Amendment was finally ratified on August 18th, 1920, allowing all American women the right to have a say in the government of their country. It is an ironic truth that, at the time, the entire country had no idea that a woman was running it. Edith Wilson would never be hailed as a hero, but like the millions of women who had kept businesses, homes, families, farms, and shops going while their men were facing the horrors of the Great War, she was instrumental in keeping America on its feet after the greatest war the world had ever seen.

The Roaring Twenties

Women's suffrage ushered in a decade of burgeoning growth and progress on almost every front. Heroes like Babe Ruth would rise in the sports world; American music would be revolutionized and truly individualized for the very first time, with legends like Louis Armstrong and Bing Crosby taking the stage; and in the industrial world, giants such as Henry Ford would emerge to boost the American economy. However, as successful as the Roaring Twenties were, they would come to an end. The Great War would soon be eclipsed by a breadth of darkness that had never before been dreamed. The Great Depression was coming—and the Second World War was right on its heels.

Chapter 15 – Disaster Strikes

Illustration V: A homeless man stands by an abandoned store in the depths of the Great Depression

Hulda Borowski could barely stand up straight. She swayed, her mind fuzzy, trying to remember which floor she worked on as a clerk in Wall Street. The elevator pinged up through the levels of the brokerage house, and Hulda stared at the numbers on the buttons, trying to make sense of them. She was so, so tired. It was almost two weeks since the Wall Street Crash had sent the economy, the nation, and the globe into a panicking tailspin, but Hulda hadn't even had a chance to be worried. Ever since Black Tuesday, the ticker counters hadn't been able to keep up with how quickly shares were being sold. The clerks, accordingly, were working overtime. More than overtime. Hulda rubbed her eyes, trying to remember the last time she'd slept. Oh, yes—in the wire room. Her boss had found her there and ordered her to go home. She must have napped there. Was it morning already? Hulda wasn't sure, but she knew that she felt utterly exhausted. She was fifty-one years old—too old for this. Too old for all of it, for the economy that she knew was about to disintegrate, for the poverty that she had heard the bankers talking about. The poverty that was coming for hundreds of thousands of Americans just like her.

It was all too much. Hulda had to do something. And at about ten o' clock that morning, she did.

She jumped off the roof, fell forty stories, and died on impact.

The Wall Street Crash of 1929

The Roaring Twenties' wild prosperity had lulled the United States into a false sense of security. As the stock market boomed and consumerism enveloped the culture into a decadent time of credit and careless spending, the entire nation was blind to the disaster that would inevitably come as a result of such excessive living. In fact, most of the world had no idea what was coming. Only a handful of Austrian and British economists dared to sound a warning bell, and they were easily brushed off. The economy had never been better. Failure wasn't even in the cards.

Except that failure, inevitably, would come. There was just too much credit in the United States, credit amassed largely by excessive spending, the new consumerist culture, and millions of dollars' worth of shares being bought on margin. Americans' optimism about the future was leading them deeper and deeper into debt. The economy could no longer support it, and so, the stock market began to decline. At first, it dipped and then rose again, wavering through the month of September. Traders brushed it aside—everyone knew that the market had its bad moments sometimes. But when Black Thursday came on October 24th, 1929, there was no more denying the fact that disaster was about to strike.

And strike it did. Despite the best efforts of investment companies and the like, Black Monday followed, the market plummeting. Black Tuesday, October 29th, was pure chaos. Over sixteen million shares were sold as panicking investors trampled over one another to get rid of their shares before they became a liability. Billions of dollars were effectively flushed down the drain. The economy had collapsed under its own weight, and while the "suicide wave" following the Wall Street Crash was largely a myth when the usual rate of suicides was blown up by the press to fuel sensationalism, there was plenty of cause for dismay. The stock market not only reeled from the punches—it fell flat. Some historians estimate that the United States lost more money in a single day during the Crash than it had spent on the entirety of WWI.

The Wall Street Crash was an unprecedented disaster of the financial world, but an even larger one would follow. Caused in part by the Crash, the Great Depression would plunge the United States into a worse condition than it had been during the throes of the First World War.

The Great Depression

President Herbert Hoover was confronted with an appalling crisis. He had been inaugurated in March 1929, becoming the president of a country whose total wealth had nearly doubled in the last decade, and he anticipated a term of peace, wealth, and luxurious excess just like what his citizens were experiencing. The Wall Street Crash, occurring only a few months after he was elected, was a rude and horrific shock. Perhaps a little in denial, Hoover told others that he expected the crisis to blow over.

It didn't. Two years after the Wall Street Crash, America was plunging deeper and deeper into an economic meltdown that would later become known as the Great Depression. Six million Americans were unemployed. By 1932, that number had risen to fifteen million. Hoover made half-hearted attempts to restore the economy by giving government loans to banks—many of which were liquidating as their clients panicked and demanded all their money back in cash—but this had little effect.

Hoover's term came to an end, and in March 1933, Franklin D. Roosevelt became president of the United States. His inauguration was a much soberer one than Hoover's; Roosevelt knew that his country was facing a crisis that had 125 million Americans looking to him for help. Things could not have looked much worse. The U.S. Treasury could not even pay its own government employees. Across the country, banks had been ordered to close as neither the banks nor their clients could afford for more banking panics to occur.

FDR himself, however, seemed to be unruffled. His manner held the calmness that Americans needed, providing an anchor in a wild storm. "The only thing we have to fear is fear itself," he told them. His personal touch immediately had a calming effect on a panicking population; addressing the people directly over the radio in his fireside chats, he made them feel a little more at ease, giving them hope that someone cared about them and was trying to help.

For many Americans, that little bit of hope was all they had. The Depression coincided with terrible droughts, which, coupled with decades of over-farming, created tremendous dust storms that enveloped the Western states with such vehemence that those states became known as the Dust Bowl. The storms drove more than half of the West's citizens to seek shelter in other states, leaving thousands of farms abandoned or foreclosed. Food production plummeted, and skyrocketing food prices combined with unemployment contributed to hideous rates of malnutrition and even death by starvation. The juggernaut that had helped to bring down Germany in the First World War was an emaciated giant now, crippled by its own excess.

Yet a new spirit was growing among the American people, one far less exuberant than the chaotic and riotous Roaring Twenties had produced. Now, with little enough to go around, Americans were learning to be more careful and to help each other. Firsthand accounts of the Depression reveal stories of kindness and selflessness even in the midst of intolerable need.

FDR seemed to share this new spirit. He instituted the New Deal, a series of efforts to stabilize the crashing economy and return peace and prosperity beneath the Star-Spangled Banner. Among the programs he put in place were the Social Security Act, providing vulnerable Americans such as children, the unemployed, and the aged with government help, and the Works Progress Administration. This administration employed more than eight million citizens to assist in endeavors that aimed to help the environment, such as planting trees and bringing fish to bodies of water.

Despite another sharp recession in 1937, the New Deal managed to scrape together a little progress, dragging the economy out of the worst of the Great Depression. This economic disaster, however, would not end until a new industry breathed life back into the American economy. Yet this new industry would not so much fix the problems as exchange one tragedy for another.

It was the industry of war. WWII had begun.

Chapter 16 – The Biggest Bomb in the World

The first bombs fell at five minutes before eight. Almost two tons of deadly explosive, it punched through the deck of the USS *Arizona*, ripping through the mighty warship and its human occupants. The sound of it echoed through the entirety of Pearl Harbor, rippling the peaceful waters of the Hawaiian bay. There was a moment of silence as the bomb rested in the ammunition magazine of the ship. Then it blew up. A fireball erupted over the harbor, reflecting in the water and in the shiny metal sides of the surrounding warships of the American Pacific Fleet. With it, over one thousand lives were vaporized, and this was only the beginning.

The sky droned and screamed with a fleet of Japanese planes. It was December 7th, 1941, and Japan had launched a surprise attack that would devastate Pearl Harbor and break millions of American hearts. Despite its reluctance to join the Second World War, the United States was about to get involved, its hand forced by the deadly attack that would be imprinted on the collective psyche of the American people forever.

U.S. Involvement in WWII

The Second World War—a war whose sheer scale of destruction would wildly eclipse the hitherto unheard-of violence of the First World War—started in 1939 when Nazi Germany first marched into Poland. It was only after the attack on Pearl Harbor in 1941, however, that the United States would enter the war.

President Franklin D. Roosevelt was not as hesitant as Wilson had been to enter the war, but he was certainly cautious. While he felt that joining the war on the Allied side was unavoidable, his administration did its best to stay out of the fight for as long as possible. Unlike the actions of the Wilson administration in WWI, FDR's government didn't sell weapons to the warring nations, nor were Americans permitted to travel with any of the countries involved in the war, preventing a second *Lusitania* from ever occurring.

The Axis, however—comprising of Germany, Italy, and Japan, all at the time fascist nations bent on expanding their empires—was determined to drag the United States into it. Anticipating an eventual conflict, FDR removed the embargo on war provisions in late 1939; by 1940, America was providing Great Britain with large amounts of resources to fuel the war effort.

It was no secret to the Axis that the United States, though officially neutral, was on the side of the Allies. The bombing of Pearl Harbor was Japan's attempt to strike first—and it worked. With a death toll of 2,403, it was a devastating attack. Yet far from crippling the United States, it drove the entire nation into a frenzy, baying for the blood of those who had killed thousands of unprepared people. The very next day, hundreds of thousands of soldiers enlisted in the U.S. Army. Together with those drafted for service overseas, they formed the American armies that would form a staunch portion of the Allied effort. The U. S. had officially sided with the Allies, joining Britain,

France, Australia, the Soviet Union, China, Canada, and South Africa, among others.

Over the next four years, more than sixteen million United States soldiers would fight in the Second World War. Efforts at home were also made and became instrumental to the Allied victory; rationing allowed the U.S. government to feed the millions of hungry mouths overseas, and vast numbers of women worked to produce what was necessary to meet the needs of both the country and army.

American heroes brought about moments of tremendous triumph in Europe, Asia, and Africa. Among the most famous was General George S. Patton, the American general who helped to win the Battle of the Bulge and yet proved spectacularly unpopular with his peers and superiors; Second Lieutenant Audie L. Murphy, responsible for 240 German deaths and the most decorated American soldier of the war; General Dwight D. Eisenhower, Supreme Allied Commander and future president of the United States; and perhaps most unusual of all, Corporal Desmond Doss, a hero of the war who never fired a single bullet. Instead, Doss was a combat medic whose faith made him a conscientious objector to any form of violence, yet he rescued more than a hundred wounded soldiers—both American and Japanese—in the face of enemy fire.

Yet none of it was enough. By May 1945, while the European theater finally saw silence as the Allied victory stilled the fighting, the Pacific was still a chaotic mess of death and destruction. Japan just wouldn't give up. Pounded relentlessly by U.S. troops, the Japanese still held firm, pouring their resources into the fighting. The war in the Pacific would cost more than a hundred thousand American lives. President Harry Truman decided in July 1945 that he would have to draw the line somewhere, and he drew it with the Potsdam Declaration, ordering Japan to surrender or face "utter destruction."

The threat was not an empty one. Truman had an ace up his sleeve that had never been seen before, a terrible evil that would end the most terribly evil war of all time at that point and change the face of warfare and the world forever. And he named it Little Boy.

The Detonation of the Atomic Bombs

The first atomic bomb in history was detonated in New Mexico on July 16th, 1945, and killed no people.

Codenamed the Gadget, the bomb was designed and built by a team of scientists and soldiers known as the Manhattan Project. FDR had been behind the formation of the team in 1942 when rumor had it that Germany was working on nuclear weapons. Now, three years later, J. Robert Oppenheimer had succeeded in building the world's first atomic bomb. Its detonation was a success, resulting in a tremendous mushroom cloud that was seen sixty miles away and produced a blast crater five feet deep and thirty feet wide.

After Japan's refusal to surrender, Truman had to make the call. It was time to end the Second World War. The detonation of the atomic bomb would cause hundreds of thousands of deaths, wipe out an entire city, and kill untold multitudes of innocent people. Yet in the face of the atrocity that was WWII, it seemed to be but a small price to pay. The war's total cost in human lives is estimated as high as 85 million. Decimating a few cities in order to end the rising death toll seemed like the only way out.

On August 6th, 1945, that apparent last resort was put into action. The Enola Gay, a B-29 U.S. bomber, soared high over Hiroshima. Did the pilot stare down out of the cockpit at the bustling city far below? Did he know that more than 300,000 people lived there? They were down there cooking, cleaning, playing with their kids, working, fighting. There were soldiers down there and men who had committed unspoken atrocities against fellow Americans. But there were also shopkeepers and accountants and doctors and policemen and paramedics and schoolchildren and housewives and...

And the sound of the Little Boy, the thin whine of it as it plummeted from the belly of the Enola Gay, whistling down toward the city.

The scope of the horrors wrought by the atomic bomb can hardly be explained in words. The cold undeniability truth of numbers serves the purpose better. 9,700 pounds: the weight of the bomb. 15,000 tons of TNT equivalent: its explosive force, fueled by uranium. 5: the number of square miles that the explosion razed to the ground. 80,000: the number of people instantly killed by the explosion, about twice the 2018 population of the country of Monaco. 300,000: the estimated number of deaths caused by Little Boy. 60: the percentage of Hiroshima's population that died from the initial explosion and the devastating radiation poisoning that would follow.

On August 9th, a second atomic bomb was dropped. This one, codename "Fat Man," was plutonium-fueled and killed about 80,000 people in the city where it was dropped—Nagasaki, Japan. The death toll was unfathomable; the landscape, destroyed; the cities, decimated. And Japan was brought, at last, to its knees. It surrendered five days after the Fat Man was detonated, ending the fighting, and the Second World War was finally and officially over on September 2nd.

The atomic bomb remains one of the most controversial topics in human history. As effective as it was at finally ending WWII, the number of innocent lives claimed in Hiroshima and Nagasaki was— and still is—viewed as an atrocity that cannot be justified. Either way, the detonation of nuclear weapons ushered in a whole new era of warfare. No longer would nations simply wade into war with one another. And in the upcoming decades, two juggernauts of international affairs would find themselves head-to-head yet unable to risk the chance of war. Because with nuclear weapons on both sides, the danger wasn't war—it was an apocalypse.

Chapter 17 – Icy Tension

The streets of Dallas, Texas were lined with an exuberant crowd that waved and cheered as the black Lincoln convertible rolled along. Seated in the open-topped limousine, President John F. Kennedy waved to the crowd, flashing a million-dollar smile. Beside him, his pretty wife Jacqueline smiled shyly; she didn't often attend his political events, but on this day, she'd decided to take a drive with her husband. It would be their last few moments together in this life.

It was November 22nd, 1963. The United States was less than twenty years out of the Second World War, and while the industry of war had revitalized its economy, Americans nonetheless found themselves living in tense times. War with the Soviet Union had been looming for years. Everyone knew that the declaration of war would mean the annihilation of millions, considering that both the Soviet Union and the U.S. possessed nuclear weapons. Already, tens of thousands of U.S. troops had been killed in Vietnam and Korea, proxy wars where the two giants battled it out while trampling upon puny innocents. Many American families had sons, brothers, husbands, or fathers fighting a war abroad even though the Second World War had only recently ended. Cinemas were filled with depictions of imagined consequences of nuclear weaponry, wanton destruction, and mutant villains in hideous costume. The Cuban

Missile Crisis of 1962 was still fresh in the minds of the people. But Kennedy had been their champion, the man who had somehow managed to negotiate his way out of nuclear war. Now they cheered him on as he soared through the streets on a tide of applause.

But not everyone was joining in on the celebration. On the sixth floor of the Texas School Book Depository, one angry American lay in wait. Lee Harvey Oswald held a Carcano M91/38 bolt action rifle with a telescopic sight. He squinted through the sight in the noonday sun, a thin trickle of sweat running down his face. A troubled young man at only 24, Oswald's mind was dark and turbulent. He'd been born the same year that the Second World War had started and endured a childhood of lack and abuse that had probably left him with profound mental illnesses. Despite this, he succeeded in becoming a U.S. Marine, but his instability led to multiple court-martials, and he eventually left the Marines in 1959.

Oswald never felt that he tasted the freedom that the United States and capitalism had promised him. So, he looked to another system and found it in the Soviet Union. Moving there directly after his discharge and renouncing his U.S. citizenship, he had worked and even married there before returning to the U.S. in 1962.

Now, he silently thanked the U.S. Marines for the one thing it had given them: training as a sharpshooter. Squinting carefully between the crosshairs, he centered his sights on the handsome face of President John F. Kennedy. Then he pulled the trigger.

The United States and the Cold War

The assassination of JFK, surrounded by controversy as it is with many theories still circulating over whether Oswald really was the lone assassin or not, was an extension of a much larger conflict in which the United States found itself shortly after the Second World War.

The landscape of international affairs had been massively changed by WWII. The mighty giant of Nazi Germany had fallen, Japan was decimated, and the victorious Allies, themselves torn after the epic war, were left to pick up the pieces. Among these Allies, two countries found themselves disagreeing profoundly on every level. While the Soviet Union had stood together with the United States to defeat the Axis, the countries could hardly have been more different. Soviet leader Joseph Stalin was a tyrant. He would exact a reign of terror over his country for more than twenty years, and his communist ways deeply chafed against the United States which had been for democracy ever since its inception. To add to this great difference, the Soviet Union blamed the U.S. for millions of Russian deaths in WWII. The Soviets believed that if the U.S. had opened a second front sooner by attacking Nazi Germany from the west, those deaths could have been prevented. Propaganda fueled both sides of the story, and by 1950, the two countries were embroiled in a silent struggle where hope to avoid conflict clashed with determination to defeat the other.

The Hot Spots of the Cold War

In any other era, the U.S. and the Soviet Union would simply have started shooting at each other. But this was post-WWII, and the stakes had changed dramatically the moment Little Boy devastated Hiroshima. Both countries were equipped with hydrogen bombs, superweapons that dwarfed the scope of the atomic bombs that had ravaged the face of Japan. Each country was equipped with weaponry that could wipe out millions, and eager as the countries were to seize each other by the throat, the memory of the destruction at Nagasaki and Hiroshima was still raw and real.

So, the Cold War was waged for about 45 years. Not a single shot was officially fired, although proxy wars popped up all over the globe as pro-Soviet Union communist nations—most notably Cuba, the U.S.' tiny but mighty neighbor just 90 miles from its Floridian coast—clashed with capitalist nations. The Soviet Union wanted to expand, and the United States did its best to thwart that expansion, engaging with communist leaders, most notably in Vietnam and Korea. Tension soared in October 1962 as the Cuban Missile Crisis revealed that Cuban communist leader, Fidel Castro, was holding Soviet nuclear weapons on his little island right on the doorstep of the U.S. Careful negotiations, however, led to the end of the crisis without nuclear detonation.

For decades, the two opponents were engaged in an arms race, each hurrying to keep up with the other, both nations knowing that if one country was more powerful than the other, then war would become inevitable—and so would defeat.

Even Germany, still reeling from the punch that had been the Allied victory, was profoundly affected by the silent struggle. The Berlin Wall was the physical manifestation of the so-called Iron Curtain, a barrier separating communist Eastern Europe with the capitalist West. It was designed to prevent oppressed citizens of East Berlin from fleeing into a place of freedom, and for decades, it caused despair to hundreds in the city.

The Space Race

Another race that the Soviet Union and the United States ran neck and neck in was the hurry to claim the final frontier of space. The Soviet Union initiated the race by launching Sputnik in 1957, the first man-made projectile to make it into orbit. Americans were both startled by the Soviets' technology and frightened by the implications of it. If they could launch a satellite into space, surely sending a nuclear warhead over to the United States would be nothing. In order to counter the Soviet Union's move, the U.S. rushed to join the race, determined to do one better: not only were American scientists going to send humans into space, but they were also going to put a man on the moon.

Once again, the Soviets beat the United States in sending a man to space for the first time. Yuri Alekseyevich Gagarin's historic flight took place on April 12th, 1961, little more than a year before the Cuban Missile Crisis. America swiftly countered by launching Alan Shepard into orbit about a month later. Attempting to boost his worried nation, JFK rashly promised that America would send a man to the moon. Although he'd been dead for almost six years by the time his promise was fulfilled, JFK wasn't wrong. Neil Armstrong and his crew famously landed on the moon on July 20th, 1969. America won the Space Race—and the Soviet Union would eventually lose the Cold War.

In 1989, Russian Premier Mikhail Gorbachev's efforts resulted in the Berlin Wall crashing down. Communism was rapidly on the decline in Eastern Europe, and the Soviet Union itself crumbled under its own weight in 1991. The Cold War was officially at an end. Today, only five communist nations remain. One of these is Cuba, the little island that almost destroyed the United States, and it remains the only communist country in the Western Hemisphere.

Chapter 18 – Freedom on the Home Front

Illustration VI: Martin Luther King Jr. delivers one of his stirring speeches

"We have been repeatedly faced with the cruel irony of watching negro and white boys on tv screens," martin luther king jr. Said, "as they kill and die together for a nation that has been unable to seat them together in the same schools."

King's words proved to be controversial, but they weren't untrue. While the united states was waging the cold war against powers that it viewed as oppressive and cruel, uncle sam himself was not innocent of restricting the freedom of some of its own citizens. Even though the country was fighting communism, it was guilty of profound racism, a fact that smacked of hypocrisy to thousands in the "land of the free" itself.

Thus began the civil rights movement that would finish what the civil war had started, 90 years after the civil war ended. It was led by a minister named martin luther king jr., and while it was supported by many whites, this time african americans would get up and fetch their freedom for themselves, following in the footsteps of the nearly 180,000 african american soldiers that had fought alongside their white fellows in the union army during the bloody civil war.

The civil rights movement

Martin luther king jr. Stared out over a rippling sea of humanity as he spoke. He had his roots in public speaking in a little baptist church in montgomery, alabama; as a minister, he'd grown comfortable addressing the public. For the past six years, as leader of the southern christian leadership conference, he'd spoken to larger and larger crowds, but this was something else. The march on washington in august 1963 had encouraged thousands of african americans to approach washington, d. C. In support of new legislation proposed by jfk. It was hoped that kennedy would pass a new civil rights act, one that would finally grant african americans the rights that they had been promised as early as the civil war.

Staring out over the vast assembly, perhaps king felt a flutter of nerves. Perhaps he was gripped, momentarily, by terror. But this minister had been fighting the giant of injustice for years—he wasn't about to let a crowd of 250,000 people scare him. Rising up, he delivered a 17-minute speech that would since be immortalized in history under the iconic title of "I have a dream." "I have a dream that one day on the red hills of georgia sons of former slaves and sons of former slave-owners will be able to sit down together at the table of brotherhood," he told them. "I have a dream that one day even in the state of mississippi, a state sweltering with the heat of injustice, sweltering with the heat of oppression, will be transformed into an oasis of freedom and justice."

Despite the fact that he himself had grown up in an affluent neighborhood of atlanta, georgia, king had been witness to the multitude of injustices still suffered by african americans. Considered as inferior to whites, they struggled under oppressive laws that allowed for segregation from the white citizens. African americans had to attend separate schools, ride separate buses, and even go to separate public toilets. They were not permitted to eat with or marry whites. Southern states—the old slave states—still clung to prejudice, embracing the slogan of "separate but equal." separation in itself would have been enough of an insult, yet when it came to equality, the slogan was nothing but an empty promise. Those facilities designated for african americans were often of much poorer quality than those given to whites. To make matters worse, african americans were treated poorly by many whites, often even with violence for no reason other than that their skin color was dark.

Rosa parks became the accidental catalyst for the civil rights movement. It was an evening in the winter of 1955 when she took her seat on the bus home from work, tired after her long day. She sat in the first row of the "colored" section of the bus, looking forward to a peaceful ride home. As the bus filled up, people were forced to stand. Noticing that white people were standing while black passengers were sitting, the bus driver moved the colored section sign back a row, ordering that rosa and the others in her row stand up. However, rosa refused to budge, and in retaliation, the bus driver called the police.

Her arrest sparked the civil rights movement, which would finally abolish segregation for good. In protest against her unfair arrest, king led a group of african american community leaders to boycott the bus system for more than a year. This forced the supreme court to put an end to segregated seating in 1956.

The new civil rights acts

President dwight d. Eisenhower signed a new civil rights act in 1957. This act made it against the law to attempt to prevent anyone from voting; while african americans were certainly still oppressed by whites, at least now it was a criminal act to stop them from having a say in whom they wanted to govern them. It was the first time that civil rights would be changed in the legislation since the reconstruction of the 1860s and 1870s.

This was progress, but still, african americans struggled under many issues, including voting literacy tests, unfair tests that african americans were forced to take for the right to vote. While many african americans did pass, often these tests were specifically rigged to be excruciatingly hard to pass, discouraging people from even attempting them. Public facilities were also still segregated. President john f. Kennedy, however, planned to change that. When he announced his intentions to work on new legislation that would reduce segregation, king jumped at the opportunity to demonstrate support for this idea. Knowing that, while king's efforts had all been solely peaceful, civil disobedience and violence had still characterized much of the civil rights movement, and he knew he needed to encourage the people to express their opinions in a peaceful manner. The march on washington succeeded in this aim.

Undoubtedly influenced by the support shown by african americans, president lyndon b. Johnson signed the civil rights act of 1964 after the death of kennedy. This act leveled the playing field by ordering public facilities to be integrated and making equal employment opportunities a requirement by law. Voting literacy tests, however, would remain until the voting rights act of 1965.

Finally—by law at least—african americans had equal opportunities. Americans of all races were free now, but martin luther king jr. Himself would hardly have any time to enjoy the newfound freedom.

He was killed on april 4th, 1968, probably by james earl ray who had racial motives for murdering king.

Chapter 19 – Terror and Its War

"I know we're all going to die," Thomas Burnett, Jr., said over the phone. "There's three of us who are going to do something about it." He paused, squeezing his eyes shut, holding his cellphone to his face in a trembling hand. The rumble of jet engines was all around him, a familiar sound that he'd heard many times during his successful career as a business executive. Yet this time he knew it was different. He knew that his words were true, yet there was no real fear in his voice. Ever since his premature birth, Thomas had known in his soul that he was going to die young, even though he was a healthy man. A pious Catholic, he was convinced that God had some spectacular plan for his life—so convinced that he and his wife, Deena, had made plans for the event of his early death.

But now, at this moment, with hijackers controlling the plane and panicking passengers around him, Thomas felt a piercing agony as he thought of Deena and their small children. "I love you, honey," he whispered. Then he put down the phone, grabbed a fire extinguisher that he held like a weapon, and walked toward the cockpit.

Minutes later, United Flight 93 plunged to the earth at more than five hundred miles per hour. The plane smashed into the dirt in a wide-open field near Shanksville, Pennsylvania, disintegrating on impact and killing the 44 people on board. Not a single person on the ground was wounded.

The same could not be said for New York City or Washington, D. C. Both of those cities were burning.

The Tragedy That Shaped a Nation

The September 11th, 2001, terrorist attacks sent a shockwave of horror all over the world. They started early that morning when 19 Islamic terrorists put into action the plan that they'd been painstakingly working on for more than a year. Osama bin Laden, leader of the terrorist group known as Al-Qaeda, was behind it all, but he wasn't actually there. The terrorists who executed the plan all knew that they were going to be killed, but they had been brainwashed thoroughly enough to believe that killing thousands of people would earn them the right to heaven.

The terrorists hijacked four planes that morning. The first crashed into the north tower of the World Trade Center, an American icon standing 110 stories tall in New York City, at 8:46 in the morning. It smashed into the building about two-thirds of the way up, and suddenly, New York was on fire. About twenty minutes later, the second plane was deliberately crashed into the south tower, and the Twin Towers burned together. Sirens filled the streets of NYC as thousands of first responders rushed to the scene.

At 9:37, a third plane was flown directly into the Pentagon in Washington, D. C. The impact ripped a gaping, burning wound in the side of the building. Soon after, Flight 93 fell out of the sky and into the Pennsylvanian field. It was obvious to Americans that this was no tragic accident—this was a deliberate attack by enemies of the United States. The aim was to spread terror and to show the military giant that it was not invincible; that without any weapons, the terrorists could take everyday objects in the life of the average American and use them to sow utter destruction on their home turf.

By the end of the attacks, almost three thousand people were dead. President George W. Bush found himself in the difficult position of having to lend a voice to a nation that was terrified, heartbroken, and shocked what it had just seen. His words, however, would characterize the American response to this terror attack. "These acts shatter steel," he said, referring to the mangled metal guts of the Twin Towers that had been shown spilling gruesomely from the ruined buildings. "But they cannot dent the steel of American resolve."

Osama bin Laden's "Letter to America," written in 2002, did little to advance his aim of terrifying the people of the United States. In it, he revealed his motive for the attacks which have gone down in history simply as "9/11." He pointed to the American culture, which was profoundly different from the extremist Islam religion that bin Laden and his followers strictly adhered to, and to America's involvement in the Middle East. The United States had been involved in the Persian Gulf War and had kept troops stationed in Saudi Arabia ever since. Considering that Mecca and Medina—places of tremendous religious significance in Islam—are located in Saudi Arabia, the presence of American troops was an insult to some of the more radical Muslims.

Bin Laden also saw America's support of the prominently Jewish country, Israel, as an affront to all of his ideologies. This all resulted in his plan to kill thousands of people who had very little to do with the war itself.

The Gulf War

The attacks of September 11th were preceded by the Gulf War, a brief but bloody conflict in which the United States once again proved itself to possess one of the most powerful military forces in the world. It all started on August 2nd, 1990, when Saddam Hussein—the dictatorial leader of Iraq—invaded the neighboring country of Kuwait with the goal of annexing its oil reserves. The United Nations was appalled by this new move by a brutal dictator and decided that the expansion of Iraqi power would have to be stopped at all costs. It banned trade with Iraq worldwide and demanded that Hussein remove his troops from Kuwait, but the Iraqi leader was adamant: he wanted Kuwait, and no amount of threats would stop him. On August 8th, he made his annexation of Kuwait official.

The U.S. and its allies responded by launching a massive operation, known as Operation Desert Shield, bringing hundreds of thousands of troops into Saudi Arabia in order to prevent Iraq from invading there as well—a war that may have had devastating consequences on the world's oil reserves. Alongside new allies from Arabia and Egypt, the U.S. then launched a two-pronged attack on Iraqi troops in Kuwait. The airborne part of the offensive was known as Operation Desert Storm; below the jets and bombers that screamed through the air and pounded the Iraqis with sophisticated explosives and missiles, Operation Desert Sabre, borne forward by American tanks, took on their enemies at ground level. The offensive began in January 1991 and proved to be far too much for Iraq to handle. The U.S. utterly overwhelmed its enemies. By February 28th, a ceasefire was called, with at least 20,000 Iraqi troops dead. The U.S. and its allies lost only about 300.

The Gulf War was another resounding victory for the United States, but the Middle East did not take kindly to this profoundly Western giant flexing its muscles so close to home. American involvement in the Gulf War was likely part of what precipitated the attacks of September 2001, and thus, this war sparked a far larger conflict that still rages today: The War on Terror.

The War on Terror

The United States has been involved in multiple overseas conflicts during the 21st century. The Gulf War was quickly followed by the Iraq War, which began in 2003 when the United States invaded Iraq to overthrow the tyrannical Saddam Hussein. This war ended in 2011 after the Iraqi Special Tribunal found Hussein guilty of crimes against humanity and hanged him in 2006.

Since October 7th, 2001, the U.S. has also been involved in a war in Afghanistan, its original operation codenamed Operation Enduring Freedom—an inspiring moniker in the wake of the September 11th attacks. While that operation has since ended, the war rages on through Operation Freedom's Sentinel. Its purpose is to deny al-Qaeda and the Taliban a safe base of operations. It can be loosely termed the Afghanistan theater of America's "War on Terror," a series of military operations launched against terrorist groups across the globe that have been raging since 9/11.

At least one important victory has already been won in the War on Terror. Almost ten years after orchestrating the attacks that devastated America and the world, Osama bin Laden was finally found hiding out in Pakistan. A group of U.S. Navy Seals was sent in to capture him, and bin Laden was killed during the attempt to arrest him. The War on Terror still goes on, but one of its leading commanders on the side of terrorism is gone for good.

The Election of the First Black President

"Tonight, we give thanks to the countless intelligence and counterterrorism professionals who've worked tirelessly to achieve this outcome," the United States president announced to his people on the evening of bin Laden's death. "The American people do not see their work, nor know their names. But tonight, they feel the satisfaction of their work and the result of their pursuit of justice."

The president who addressed the people on the night of May 2nd, 2011, to announce that Osama bin Laden was killed was President Barack Obama. Not only had he been a Nobel Peace Prize laureate in 2009, but Obama was also the first African American president ever to be elected. In 2008—143 years after slavery was abolished and 44 years after Martin Luther King Jr. at last won his fight for equality—Obama was elected president of the United States. Less than a century and a half before, African Americans had labored beneath the snapping whips and brutal words of overseers; now, an African American was sworn in as president. Despite the chaos in the U.S. and the world, one beacon of progress at least shone through the smoke of 9/11.

Conclusion

Nobody can deny that the United States is a big place. Considering that the United Kingdom can fit into the area of the U.S. about 40 times, the sheer area of the country is impressive, and its diversity even more so. Yet the U.S. is not large only in size but in everything it does: its wars, its successes, its epic blunders, its individuality, its willingness to set a trend, its courageous ability to go against the status quo in the name of freedom, its spirit of entrepreneurship, and its capacity for invention and innovation.

The United States has undeniably been one of the most influential countries in the world. From its books and movies to its multitude of inventions, the U.S. has seeped its way into the collective consciousness of most of the modern world. In fact, despite the fact that the U.S. has vociferously advocated against expansionism for more than a century, it's not unfair to say that its culture has taken over much of the world. The United States hasn't added to its considerable girth since Hawaii's admission in 1959, yet somehow, it's everywhere.

Everyone who has ever turned on an electric light bulb, flown in an airplane, ridden in a Ford car, said the word "OK," been on Facebook, or watched a movie has sipped from the deep well of

American innovation. This looming giant has made its share of mistakes, inspiring criticism from many different quarters all over the world, yet everyone knows exactly where they were on 9/11. Anyone old enough to remember can recall the moment when they heard about the first plane that crashed into that north tower on that fateful morning.

There have been centuries of struggle. There have been bloody defeats and tremendous victories. Heroes and villains have risen up and struggled over enormous issues that sometimes the rest of the world has refused to face. Through revolution and civil war, through protest and depression, through colonization and tragedy, all the way from the Lost Colony to the War on Terror, the United States has emerged: a military juggernaut, a cultural trendsetter, and above all, the land of the free. The home of the brave.

Here are some other Captivating History books that you might be interested in

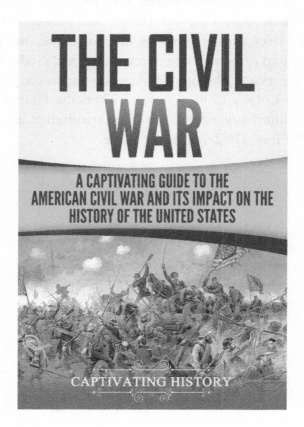

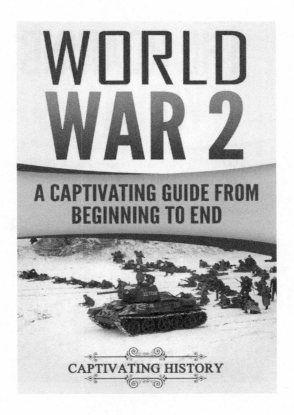

THE ROARING TWENTIES

A CAPTIVATING GUIDE TO A PERIOD OF DRAMATIC SOCIAL AND POLITICAL CHANGE, A FALSE SENSE OF PROSPERITY AND ITS IMPACT ON THE GREAT DEPRESSION

CAPTIVATING HISTORY

AFRICAN
AMERICAN
HISTORY

A CAPTIVATING GUIDE TO THE PEOPLE AND EVENTS
THAT SHAPED THE HISTORY OF THE UNITED STATES

CAPTIVATING HISTORY

Sources

http://www.crystalinks.com/nativeamcreation.html

https://prezi.com/ykvfzcomwc0e/chinook-creation-myth/

https://prezi.com/3kcshnvcqfdt/chinook-creation-myth/

https://www.cleveland.com/expo/life-and-culture/erry-2018/10/71b738640b7079/ohios-serpent-mound-an-archaeo.html

https://www.smithsonianmag.com/history/the-clovis-point-and-the-discovery-of-americas-first-culture-3825828/

https://www.infoplease.com/us/race-population/major-pre-columbian-indian-cultures-united-states

https://www.census.gov/history/pdf/c2010br-10.pdf

https://www.scholastic.com/teachers/articles/teaching-content/history-native-americans/

https://www.historyonthenet.com/native-americans-origins

https://www.history.com/topics/exploration/john-cabot

https://www.history.com/this-day-in-history/ponce-de-leon-discovers-florida

https://fcit.usf.edu/florida/lessons/de_leon/de_leon1.htm

https://www.washingtonpost.com/news/answer-
sheet/wp/2013/10/14/christopher-columbus-3-things-you-think-he-
did-that-he-didnt/?noredirect=on&utm_term=.e921b34a7cfcme

https://exploration.marinersmuseum.org/subject/jacques-cartier/

https://www.historytoday.com/archive/months-past/birth-amerigo-
vespucci

https://www.u-s-history.com/pages/h1138.html

http://mentalfloss.com/article/560395/facts-about-sir-walter-raleigh

https://www.nationalgeographic.com/magazine/2018/06/lost-colony-
roanoke-history-theories-croatoan/

https://www.history.com/news/what-happened-to-the-lost-colony-of-
roanoke

http://mentalfloss.com/article/69358/8-most-intriguing-
disappearances-history

http://www.let.rug.nl/usa/outlines/history-1994/early-america/the-
first-europeans.php

Illustration   I:
https://commons.wikimedia.org/wiki/File:Dugout_canoe_manner_bo
ats_de_bry.jpg

https://newsmaven.io/indiancountrytoday/archive/the-true-story-of-
pocahontas-historical-myths-versus-sad-reality-
WRzmVMu47E6Guz0LudQ3QQ/

http://www.americaslibrary.gov/jb/colonial/jb_colonial_subj.html

https://www.history.com/topics/colonial-america/thirteen-colonies

https://www.texasgateway.org/resource/exploration-and-
colonization-america

http://www.loc.gov/teachers/classroommaterials/presentationsandact
ivities/presentations/timeline/colonial/

https://www.history.com/this-day-in-history/the-pilgrim-wampanoag-peace-treaty

https://www.uswars.net/king-georges-war/

https://www.mountvernon.org/george-washington/french-indian-war/washington-and-the-french-indian-war/

https://www.mountvernon.org/george-washington/french-indian-war/ten-facts-about-george-washington-and-the-french-indian-war/

https://www.history.com/topics/native-american-history/french-and-indian-war

https://www.history.com/topics/american-revolution/boston-massacre

http://www.ushistory.org/declaration/related/massacre.html

https://www.britannica.com/event/Boston-Tea-Party

https://www.history.com/topics/american-revolution/boston-tea-party

http://www.eyewitnesstohistory.com/teaparty.htm

https://www.ducksters.com/history/american_revolution/intolerable_acts.php

http://www.ushistory.org/us/9g.asp

https://www.poets.org/poetsorg/poem/paul-reveres-ride

https://www.history.com/news/11-things-you-may-not-know-about-paul-revere

https://www.history.com/topics/american-revolution/battles-of-lexington-and-concord

https://www.britannica.com/event/Battles-of-Saratoga

https://www.history.com/topics/american-revolution/declaration-of-independence

https://www.britishbattles.com/war-of-the-revolution-1775-to-1783/battle-of-yorktown/

https://www.history.com/this-day-in-history/battle-of-yorktown-begins

https://www.battlefields.org/learn/articles/overview-american-revolutionary-war

https://www.history.com/topics/american-revolution/american-revolution-history

http://sageamericanhistory.net/federalperiod/topics/national1783_89.html

http://avalon.law.yale.edu/18th_century/washing.asp

http://www.ushistory.org/us/17d.asp

https://www.britannica.com/biography/George-Washington/Presidency

https://www.mountvernon.org/george-washington/the-first-president/election/10-facts-about-washingtons-election/

https://www.biography.com/people/george-washington-9524786

https://www.history.com/news/what-was-the-xyz-affair

https://www.americanhistorycentral.com/entries/quasi-war/

https://www.smithsonianmag.com/smart-news/unremembered-us-france-quasi-war-shaped-early-americas-foreign-relations-180963862/

https://2001-2009.state.gov/r/pa/ho/time/nr/16318.htm

http://www.historicships.org/constellation.html

https://www.history.com/topics/war-of-1812/battle-of-new-orleans

https://www.britannica.com/event/War-of-1812

https://www.smithsonianmag.com/history/the-10-things-you-didnt-know-about-the-war-of-1812-102320130/

https://www.history.com/topics/native-american-history/trail-of-tears

https://www.britannica.com/topic/Indian-Removal-Act

https://www.pbs.org/wgbh/aia/part4/4p2959.html

https://www.history.com/news/native-americans-genocide-united-states

http://www.ushistory.org/us/24f.asp

https://cherokee.org/About-The-Nation/History/Trail-of-Tears/A-Brief-History-of-the-Trail-of-Tears

https://www.britannica.com/event/Second-Seminole-War

https://www.thoughtco.com/second-seminole-war-2360813

https://fcit.usf.edu/florida/lessons/sem_war/sem_war1.htm

https://www.sermonsearch.com/sermon-outlines/21975/confidence-in-prayer/

https://www.u-s-history.com/pages/h1091.html

http://www.ushistory.org/us/22c.asp

https://www.pbs.org/wgbh/americanexperience/features/goldrush-california/

https://www.history.com/topics/westward-expansion/gold-rush-of-1849

https://www.historynet.com/california-gold-rush

https://www.britannica.com/event/assassination-of-Abraham-Lincoln

http://www.abrahamlincolnonline.org/lincoln/speeches/gettysburg.htm

https://www.history.com/topics/american-civil-war/battle-of-gettysburg

https://www.battlefields.org/learn/articles/brief-overview-american-civil-war

https://www.history.com/topics/american-civil-war/american-civil-war-history

https://www.history.com/topics/19th-century/bleeding-kansas

https://www.britannica.com/topic/Ku-Klux-Klan

https://www.history.com/topics/american-civil-war/reconstruction

https://www.britannica.com/topic/Civil-Rights-Act-United-States-1875

https://www.britannica.com/topic/Wounded-Knee-Massacre

https://www.thoughtco.com/about-the-native-american-ghost-dance-4125921

https://www.history.com/topics/native-american-history/wounded-knee

https://www.history.com/topics/native-american-history/battle-of-the-little-bighorn

https://www.history.com/news/10-things-you-didnt-know-about-the-old-west

https://www.thevintagenews.com/2017/12/31/wild-west-era-2/

https://www.loc.gov/rr/hispanic/1898/intro.html

https://www.britannica.com/event/Spanish-American-War

https://www.businessinsider.com/major-battles-fought-by-the-us-during-world-war-i-2018-11?IR=T#after-a-decisive-allied-victory-germans-accept-defeat-and-sign-for-peace-10

https://www.nationalgeographic.com/archaeology-and-history/magazine/2017/03-04/world-war-i-united-states-enters/

https://www.thoughtco.com/second-battle-of-the-marne-2361412

https://www.britannica.com/event/Second-Battle-of-the-Marne

https://www.wearethemighty.com/history/this-is-why-the-3rd-infantry-division-is-called-rock-of-the-marne

https://www.history.com/topics/womens-history/19th-amendment-1

https://www.pbs.org/newshour/health/woodrow-wilson-stroke

https://www.archives.gov/publications/prologue/1998/fall/military-service-in-world-war-one.html

https://www.history.com/topics/great-depression/1929-stock-market-crash

http://www.american-historama.org/1929-1945-depression-ww2-era/causes-wall-street-crash.htm

http://www.newworldencyclopedia.org/entry/Wall_Street_Crash_of_1929

https://www.washingtonpost.com/archive/opinions/1987/10/25/the-jumpers-of-29/17defff9-f725-43b7-831b-7924ac0a1363/?utm_term=.0d663d5ecc79

http://voices.washingtonpost.com/washingtonpostinvestigations/2009/01/the_wall_street_leap.html

http://professorbuzzkill.com/the-men-who-jumped-during-the-stock-market-crash-of-1929-2/

https://www.history.com/topics/great-depression/great-depression-history

https://www.thebalance.com/the-great-depression-of-1929-3306033

https://www.npr.org/templates/story/story.php?storyId=97468008

https://www.thoughtco.com/great-depression-pictures-1779916

https://www.history.com/topics/world-war-ii/pearl-harbor

https://247wallst.com/special-report/2018/05/25/most-decorated-war-heroes/2/

http://www.pwencycl.kgbudge.com/C/a/Casualties.htm

https://www.atomicheritage.org/history/bombings-hiroshima-and-nagasaki-1945

https://www.atomicheritage.org/history/little-boy-and-fat-man

https://www.history.com/topics/world-war-ii/atomic-bomb-history

https://www2.gwu.edu/~erpapers/teachinger/glossary/world-war-2.cfm

https://www.thoughtco.com/overview-of-world-war-ii-105520

https://www.history.com/topics/cold-war/cold-war-history

https://www.britannica.com/event/Cold-War

https://www.google.com/search?q=assassination+of+jfk+cold+war&ie=utf-8&oe=utf-8

https://www.history.com/this-day-in-history/john-f-kennedy-assassinated

https://www.psychologytoday.com/us/blog/evil-deeds/201311/why-did-lee-harvey-oswald-kill-john-fitzgerald-kennedy

https://www.history.com/topics/cold-war/berlin-wall

https://www.history.com/topics/black-history/martin-luther-king-jr

https://www.history.com/topics/black-history/civil-rights-movement

https://www.inc.com/jeff-haden/two-of-greatest-martin-luther-king-jr-speeches-youve-never-heard.html

https://www.archives.gov/files/press/exhibits/dream-speech.pdf

https://www.nzherald.co.nz/world/news/article.cfm?c_id=2&objectid=12093351

https://www.history.com/topics/21st-century/9-11-attacks

https://patch.com/california/sanramon/were-going-to-do-something-remembering-thomas-burnett-jr

https://www.britannica.com/biography/Barack-Obama/Politics-and-ascent-to-the-presidency

http://edition.cnn.com/2011/WORLD/asiapcf/05/02/bin.laden.announcement/index.html

Illustration II: By Copy of lithograph by Sarony & Major, 1846 - This media is available in the holdings of the National Archives and Records Administration, cataloged under the National Archives Identifier (NAID) 532892., Public Domain, https://commons.wikimedia.org/w/index.php?curid=112653

Illustration III: By John Trumbull - Winterthur Museum, Public Domain, https://commons.wikimedia.org/w/index.php?curid=57115499

Illustration IV: https://commons.wikimedia.org/wiki/California_Gold_Rush#/media/File:SanFranciscoharbor1851c_sharp.jpg

Illustration V: By Dorothea Lange - Franklin D. Roosevelt Presidential Library and Museum (53227(292), 00/00/1935, 27-0621a.gif), Public Domain, https://commons.wikimedia.org/w/index.php?curid=4275764

Illustration VI: By O. Fernandez, New York World-Telegram and the Sun staff photographer - Library of Congress Prints and Photographs Division. New York World-Telegram and the Sun Newspaper Photograph Collection. http://hdl.loc.gov/loc.pnp/cph.3c11157, Public Domain, https://commons.wikimedia.org/w/index.php?curid=1307066